PARALLELS AND ACTUALS OF POLITICAL DEVELOPMENT

Also by A.H. Somjee

VOTING BEHAVIOUR IN AN INDIAN VILLAGE
POLITICAL THEORY OF JOHN DEWEY
DEMOCRACY AND POLITICAL CHANGE IN VILLAGE
INDIA
DEMOCRATIC PROCESS IN A DEVELOPING SOCIETY
POLITICAL CAPACITY IN DEVELOPING SOCIETIES
POLITICAL SOCIETY IN DEVELOPING COUNTRIES

PARALLELS AND ACTUALS OF POLITICAL DEVELOPMENT

A. H. Somjee

MACMILLAN
PRESS

JF
60
.S65
1986

© A. H. Somjee 1986

First published 1986

Published by
THE MACMILLAN PRESS LTD
Houndmills, Basingstoke, Hampshire RG21 2XS
and London
Companies and representatives
throughout the world

Printed in Hong Kong

British Library Cataloguing in Publication Data
Somjee, A. H.
Parallels and actuals of political development.
1. Developing countries—Politics and government
I. Title
320.9172'4   JF60
ISBN 0-333-39698-7

Contents

Preface

In our examination of the political societies of developing countries, we are often inclined to go in search of parallels of historical and political experiences of Western countries. And when we do not notice such parallels, we tend to regard what we see as obdurately traditional or deviant from the norm set by us. What we do not examine, however, are the actualities of political complexity in the relatively less familiar situations of the non-Western world. Apart from the near absence of scholarly criticism and controversy, which are the idioms through which human knowledge advances, such an approach – looking for parallels rather than actuals – has been forced upon us by the nature of our theoretical knowledge in the subdiscipline of political development. Such a body of knowledge, which is entirely based on the political experiences of a few Western countries, despite its fundamental contribution, needs to be refined, supplemented and in some cases reformulated, so as to be able to justify its claim to universal validity. This book seeks to identify some of those inadequacies, insensitivities and distortions caused by various theoretical approaches and conceptual tools used, in order to understand the social and political reality of the non-Western world.

In the corpus of theoretical knowledge used to understand political development, certain assumptions are made with regard to a parallel development in the political societies of emerging countries. We assume that despite reverses and setbacks when those societies politically mature, over decades and centuries, their development too will be in the direction which has been already traversed by Western political societies. Such an argument presupposes an empty cultural space within which forces of modernisation, the Western state system, borrowed political ideals and emulated institutions and practices operate. That view is erroneous. What it ignores is the fact that the forces of history, culture and tradition vitally influence perceptions of social reality and predispositions to individual and group action within each society. What is more, they also influence and shape the meaning and operations of borrowed political ideals and public institutions.

Without subscribing to an extreme position of cultural deter-
minism, we need to know what actually happens to transplanted legal
and political institutions and the quality of public life to which they
give rise. In other words, we need to go beyond the exercise of identifying parallel institutional practices and public behaviours, within
political societies which have come under the influence of more politically developed ones, to the actualities of their institutional operations and the complexities of their public life in general.

Such a shift of emphasis, however, is not without its own problems. This is because the very tools of conceptual inquiry, analysis,
explanation and reportage that we use for such purposes bring in
their own biases, which in turn distort our perspectives on the problem of understanding the actualities of those political societies.
Among the social scientists, anthropologists, who, like students of
political development, do their research in developing societies, have
grappled with the problem of Western bias from the very inception
of their discipline, and have deliberately kept alive the controversy
surrounding relativism and universalism as a continuing warning
against the possibility of such a bias.

Such biases, as we shall see, go beyond the problems of intellectual 'selectivity', which are unavoidable. The biases referred to in
this book are of a different nature. They constrain us, more often
than not, from going beyond the search for parallels, and thereby
restrict our understanding of the social and political reality of developing societies to those areas which outwardly, formally, vaguely or even
deceptively resemble our own. The rest is consigned to the realm
of the unessential, and therefore remains unexplored.

There is, then, a built-in insensitivity, in a number of theories of
social change and political development, to what happens to the various transplanted social and political institutions, ideals and practices even when they have to function within a culturally different
environment. Such theories often take for granted that the borrowed
institutions and practices will, sooner or later, with or without minor
cultural differences, be able to recreate social and political conditions which are similar to those in the countries from where they were
borrowed.

Max Weber in his writings had warned students of society and
politics of a possible fallacy of emanationism, as Nisbet called it, in
such an approach. His example was that of the growth of capitalism together with various legal and political institutions associated
with it. For him, capitalism did not automatically emanate from

feudalism. In the growth of capitalism, along with a liberal state, permissive of its entrepreneurial activity and a participatory citizenship, there was the fortuitous configuration of several historical circumstances. And in several other countries, different versions of capitalism did not automatically give rise to legal and political institutions similar to those in Western Europe. He therefore emphasised repeatedly the need to cultivate sensitivity to what actually happened in history rather than guess about it with the help of a neat theory.

In addition to the problem of sensitivity, the corpus of theoretical knowledge that we use in the study of political development also lacks an assimilative disposition and effort. Instead of trying to understand the non-Western world, first of all, in its own historical and cultural contexts, and then in the contexts of those public concerns which are truly universal, it often tries to concentrate on certain abstracted aspects of political societies which can be conveniently fitted into its efforts to validate universally some of its untested speculative theories and models. Whatever the political societies of the developing world have to offer, by way of their uniqueness or potential universal value, is rarely assimilated into such knowledge. Consequently, instead of incrementally and cumulatively expanded theoretical knowledge, incorporating into its main body the universal significance of what other cultures have to offer, with all the necessary refinements and reformulations which such incorporations would involve, what we have is a dubiously claimed universal validity of knowledge which is largely grounded in our own social and political experience. We shall illustrate this problem by taking a few examples of the conceptual inadequacy of such a body of knowledge in understanding and explaining certain complexities of the three major multilayered political societies of Asia, namely, India, China and Japan.

Finally, our emphasis on the need to consider the context-dependent aspects of various institutional transplants and emulated ideals and practices, which have to function within different cultural situations and historical experiences, will no doubt push us in the direction of relativism. This in fact has happened to anthropologists with their research interests in developing societies. They often subscribe to various versions and degrees of relativism. But students of political development cannot afford to subscribe to positions of relativism in all areas of their intellectual concern. Since they deal with matters relating to human political development, with its ability to seek responses and demand accountability of those in public office, and, above all, with the quality of public life in general, all of universal concern, they have to exclude relativistic explanations and judgements from these vital areas. Such concerns force them to take universalistic positions regardless of concessions to relativistic positions in understanding context-dependent aspects of public life in some other areas. This is because issues such as the rule of law, electorally mandated political authority, independent judiciary, due process, freedom of speech, etc., cannot be explained away, or their absence condoned, with the help of cultural relativism.

Some of these vital matters of public concern are derived or inferred solely from the political ideals and experiences of Western countries. While the political experiences of some of the countries of the West have been archetypal experiences, they need to be supplemented. Scholars are now beginning to look at what can also be added as values of universal significance which have originated from non-Western sources.

All this will give rise to a position of curious dualism: of the need to emphasise a relativistic position in order to understand the actuals of political experiences and problems of different societies; and of the need to have a universalistic position, on what I have called 'the public minimum', so as to guarantee civilised political life regardless of cultural and historical background. Such a dualistic position, with which we live comfortably in the existential world, will no doubt invite criticism from the point of view of logical inconsistency, the problem of jurisdiction, the danger of rationalisation and self-deception. Nevertheless, it is an area which, with all its potential for controversy, needs to be explored further.

Within the subdiscipline of political development, we are passing through a period of nemesis of hypermodelling. We have rarely submitted our models, and theoretical knowledge in general, to rigorous historical and empirical testing. And our explorations into development theory have been, by and large, misinformed and misconceived. To resuscitate them, we need to know what went wrong.

The present volume seeks to raise these and other related issues by critiquing certain approaches and biases of development theories. We all cut our analytical teeth by biting into the flesh of our elders. And we also hope that such a bite will be regarded by them as a part of our intellectual growing up.

Although I am of Asian origin, I have now spent a major portion of my professional life in Canada, Britain and the United States. Consequently, I too share a number of the intellectual perspectives and limitations of Western scholars who are engaged in examining non-Western societies. In that sense, the present work is an exercise in self-criticism. The fact that I put on two hats is incidental to this work. My dissatisfaction with our theoretical knowledge is almost entirely based on my difficulty in using it while doing my longitudinal research in rural and urban India.

I am grateful to the Warden of Nuffield College, Oxford, for allowing me to be a part of its scholarly community during the Trinity Term of 1983. I am equally grateful to Harvard University for giving me the status of a Visiting Scholar during the academic year of 1983–4. My grateful thanks are due to the Director and Fellows of the Center for International Affairs at Harvard for a stimulating year which helped shape many of my ideas. I am also grateful to the Social Sciences and Humanities Research Council of Canada for a leave fellowship during that academic year.

The librarians and staff of Simon Fraser University, Oxford and Harvard were most helpful in providing facilities for my work. My secretary, Margaret Paine, was most helpful in sorting out so many of my papers connected with research for this book, and Barbara Barnett helped me with the word-processing of the manuscript. My wife, Geeta, imposed the strictest possible standard for attaining clarity in a work of this nature, where simplicity of argument and presentation are often the first victims. For whatever shortcomings which remain in this book, I alone am responsible.

A.H. Somjee

Grasse
France

1 Assumed Universals of Political Development

In various writings on political development, a number of assumptions are often made which imply that regardless of the presence of the factors of culture, history and tradition, the political evolution of developing societies will, sooner or later, follow the direction already laid down by the industrialised societies of the West. Such a view of their evolutionary course, largely extrapolated from the historical experiences of a few Western societies, is seen as inescapable for developing countries. An intellectual position of this nature, with a number of assumptions of its own, was constantly reinforced by a growing body of theoretical knowledge, from Auguste Comte to Gabriel Almond. Although this corpus of theoretical knowledge, which is almost entirely rooted in the social and political experiences of the Western world, did acknowledge the cultural peculiarities of different societies, it nevertheless foresaw the drift of their future evolutionary course, with reverses and setbacks, in a direction that was similar, if not identical, to that of the countries of the West. Advanced industrialised societies were viewed by it as 'leader societies', and developing countries as 'follower societies'. It was generally assumed that in following the lead of industrialised societies, especially in the fields of science, technology, education, legal and political institutions, and in building the infrastructure of a modern state, developing countries too will undergo a social and political change which will, eventually, make them look like the countries of the West.

In making such universalistic assumptions, the body of theoretical knowledge in political development was encouraged by two major factors. First, by the unanimous adoption of the Western state system by the non-Western countries in order to transact their business internationally and, with some qualifications, nationally. Second, the exposure of the elite from developing countries to Western education and social and political ideals, and their commitments and

1

efforts to establish corresponding social and political institutions in
their own countries in the post-colonial period.

Within the developing countries themselves, such an imitative
course of development had been in progress prior to the termination of colonial rule and then, at a much more accelerated pace, under
the stewardship of their nationalist leaders. The latter superimposed
a large number of educational, administrative, legal and political
institutions, imitated and adapted from the West, on their indigenous
social organisations.

What has escaped our attention, however, is the cultural contexts
within which such borrowed institutions and practices had to operate. Such institutions, wherever they have survived, have demonstrated their differences in spirit, mode of operation and, above all,
in the quality of public life which emanates from them. The question, then, is whether we should continue to look at such differences
as parallel to some of the historical phases in the evolution of public
institutions in the West, or take a hard look at such differences and
thereby reach a more realistic understanding of their actualities?

In this chapter I shall argue that because of certain of our universalistic assumptions we are often unable to identify the essential difference which the social and cultural background of developing countries
has made to what they borrowed from the West; unless we become
aware of such differences we will be unable to evaluate the performance of their institutions and the quality of public life which they
provide.

Here we have an additional problem: our cognitive approaches
in examining these societies are themselves not free from certain limit-
ing and distorting biases. Such biases, as we shall see, go beyond the
confines of intellectual selectivity.[1] And they, along with our universalistic assumptions about development, distort our understanding
of the actualities of the development process itself.

This chapter is divided into the following parts: (i) perceptual and
conceptual bias; (ii) value bias; (iii) reductionist bias; (iv) diffusionist
bias; and (v) anthropologists and the problem of Western bias. We
shall now examine each of these points in some detail.

I   PERCEPTUAL AND CONCEPTUAL BIAS

Our perceptual and conceptual bias, in viewing and analysing developing societies, has often limited or distorted our understanding of the

actualities of those societies. In his *Embattled Reason*, Reinhard Bendix remarked that in a period when so many new political societies have come into existence, especially after the Second World War – with different cultural backgrounds and problems of their own – the intellectual tools that we use to understand them belong to past periods.[2] Consequently, we have shown much less sensitivity to the actualities of social and political life in those societies and to the complexities of continuing change in them. Even when we do identify them, we often seek to explain them in terms of the historical social and political experiences of Western Europe and North America. In our perceptual and conceptual explanations, therefore, we often seem to make universalistic assumptions, despite our routine pronouncements to the contrary, as to the unilinear course of development of all societies once they become involved in the process of modernisation. The process of modernisation, we assume, is expected to do to them and their cultures what it did to the countries of Western Europe and North America. Moreover, and more significantly, we assume that the social consequences of such a process will be similar everywhere and explainable with the help of the body of theoretical knowledge already developed to explain change in Western countries.

With the discovery of different lands and the conquest of most of them, from the fifteenth to the eighteenth centuries, European scholars needed a theory not only classifying peoples and cultures but also describing what would happen to those who were supposed to be 'inferior' to Europeans, in terms of their rational property. Voltaire, for instance, gloated over the fact that Western humanity, through progress and rational development, had demonstrated its superiority and advance over the rest. Other scholars were inclined to view different segments of humanity as being at different stages in the march of progress. Nevertheless, in the centre of global evolution there was the unmistakable assumption of 'western history as *the* history of humanity and the image of humanity's future'.[3] So far as other cultures, including classical cultures, were concerned, they were either consigned to the category of 'unhistorical'[4] or considered to be of not much consequence anyway. Later on, Karl Marx, the universalistic economic historian, even saw virtue in the colonisation of India by Britain, for, according to him, through the exploitative imperial rule India would be able to get rid of her divisions of caste and fragmentary village system and would then be ushered into a period of modernity, ready to enter into a capitalist phase and its inevitable climax of a classless society.[5]

On either side of the ideological divide of the nineteenth and twen-tieth centuries, social theorists have been inclined to treat the tradi-tional organisations of emerging societies as some kind of *hard shell*,[6] which has to be broken into smithereens before they can be modernised. Thus Marx on one side, and liberal social theorists on the other, came out with a variety of explanations characterising developing countries with similar problems and solutions.

To Marx, developing countries can see glimpses of their own future in the developed countries. In his words: 'The country that is more developed industrially only shows to the less developed, the image of its own future.'[7]

The peculiarities of culture and tradition, deeply assimilated by people, were of little consequence to Marx. For him, these were mere reflections in people's thinking of certain modes of production, and were bound to be replaced by a modern culture when those societies industrialised themselves. For him, therefore, the essential social con-sequence of modes of production was the same everywhere.

The liberal thinkers, on the other hand, were inclined to treat tradi-tional societies as transitional, the dynamics of which had suffered setbacks because of the inhibiting rather than permissive nature of their social structures, until they finally became victims of colonial-ism. But there again, they felt that those self-paralysing social struc-tures, and their manifold practices, would give way once modern education and contact with the West increased. At some stage, they hoped, the leaders of transitional societies would grasp the desira-bility of modernising themselves on the lines of industrialised soci-eties and thereby restore their own lost dynamism.

While the liberal thinkers remained quite explicit on the disap-pearance of the vestiges of traditionalism, they vaguely entertained the possibility of the survival of some of the cultural aspects as a thin icing on the modern core of developing societies.

Such assumptions of Western social theorists were not borne out by the three major political societies of Asia: Japan, a highly tech-nologised society; China, a society with a highly externally disciplined labour force; and India, a society making a conscious attempt to hasten the pace of social change within a democratic framework. These countries, in their attempt to force the pace of their own development, did not, and could not, fully give up the traditional cultural bases of their respective societies. Their modernisation processes consisted of large-scale or select borrowings and emula-tions of technology, organisation, education, institutions of law and politics, bureaucracy, means of communication and transport. While such borrowings did make a considerable difference to the original character of these societies, they nevertheless retained, or could not shake off, a large number of their own indigenous features, which subsequently influenced the operation of those institutions and practices they had emulated from elsewhere.

What was overlooked by the social theorists of the nineteenth and twentieth centuries, therefore, was the essential *permeability* of these societies – and for that matter of any society. Instead of acting as hard shells, which, as the modernisation theorists assumed, had to be broken, these societies acted like *sponges*, absorbing whatever they wanted. In such a process, some things were absorbed more due to contact and exposure rather than through conscious choice. Nevertheless, it was not watchfulness and selectivity that restricted the form and content of what was absorbed but precisely those elements which the borrowing societies could absorb with minimum friction without altering their essential nature, which had been there culturally over the millennia. Thus, despite large-scale borrowing and emulation the societies of Japan, China and India have retained their own complex cultural bases sufficiently to influence and colour the operations of institutions and practices which they absorbed from outside. Later on, we shall examine in detail some of the peculiar characteristics of their political institutions.

These societies, which became or are becoming 'modern' without becoming 'Western', present new problems in terms of understanding their social and political development in their own terms as well as in terms which are universally applicable. Consequently, a corpus of theoretical knowledge, which is premised on the assumption of the total disappearance of the indigenous component of traditional societies, in the process of their own development, has become highly inadequate. For what is assumed in such an argument is that whenever a country tries to industrialise itself, the social and political concomitants[8] which inevitably follow will eradicate differences between different societies. By the same token, the greater the number of countries taking to modernisation, the greater the applicability of the existing theoretical knowledge.

The intellectual effort which such a basic universalistic assumption embodied viewed traditional societies in a teleological movement, with a common direction and standard pattern already set by a select number of Euro-american societies. It was with reference to them that other societies had to be characterised and classified.

Whatever prevailed, historically speaking, in a select number of Western societies was rationalised, and universally applicable standards were drawn from them in order to evaluate and judge other societies. On the face of it, it appeared to be a Cartesian exercise in pure rationality, with universal applicability, but in fact the sensitivity and relevance of such standards did not go beyond the historical experiences of a few countries.

Since the liberal political development of Britain, France and the United States, spread over nearly 300 years, took place as a result of a thrust towards economic modernisation for profit under capitalism, its accompanying emphasis on the rights of the individual, and the kind of legal and political institutions which were permissive of the exercise of such rights, came to be identified as crucial factors in economic modernisation. From the very start, therefore, such a notion of economic modernisation, based on the historical experiences of a few societies, was raised to the level of a universal standard with which to judge other societies, Western as well as non-Western. Barrington Moore Jr in political economy, and Talcott Parsons in social organisation, provided theoretical criteria, based on the experiences of countries which went through early capitalism and its accompanying fierce individualism, to determine the nature and quality of other societies which could not go through a similar or corresponding experience for historical reasons. While Moore provided the model of two sets of actors, i.e. landed gentry and peasantry,[9] and their different kinds of cooperation and conflict, Parsons provided his theory of 'pattern variables'[10] to act as a ready reckoner to determine how far certain societies had progressed towards economic and political modernisation.

This was then followed by theories of 'stages' of growth and development, both economic and political, at the hands of Rostow[11] and Organski,[12] and a highly self-confident theory of sequences of urbanisation, literacy, communication and competitive politics formulated by Lerner.[13] All these thinkers saw the 'global' relevance of what the countries of the West went through. The climax of this line of thinking was reached when Banks and Textor provided an 'attribute checklist' to mark off characteristics of countries as 'modern' or 'non-modern'.[14] Once again, the notion of 'attributes' was based exclusively on Western experience. The scholars engaged in preparing them did not worry about the extent of their applicability to other societies.

Even certain major attempts to study developing countries, but by no means all of them, invariably started off with the help of 'theoretical models', grounded in the social and political experiences of a handful of Western countries. A number of these were cognitive exercises in validating a previously arrived at grand theory, or seeking support for deductions made therefrom,[15] rather than refining that theory at the end of one's research. In the social sciences, only in recent years have scholars begun to see their role not merely as validators but as questioners and refiners of the previously arrived at theories. Simultaneously, they have also started questioning the simplistic classification of societies into 'traditional' and 'modern'. With the questioning of such a classification there are also questions directed at the body of theoretical knowledge, and those assumptions that rationalised it. Later on we shall examine in detail the increasing awareness of scholars of the inadequacy of such knowledge for understanding the actualities of the development processes of emerging countries.

II VALUE BIAS

Most of the value biases, in either understanding or explaining political development, also centre around the mistaken polarity of 'tradition' and 'modernity'. 'Modernity' – with some justifiable claims to economic, industrial and, in some cases, political advancement – was allowed to become a means of self-adulation, superiority, lead position and prescription for replication in *all* walks of life. The benefaction provided by 'modernity', in all walks of life for everyone, was always assumed. At the other extreme, 'traditional', as a shorthand term for backwardness in all compartments of life, was also taken for granted and its drawbacks were considered to be unworthy even of any systematic examination. Research efforts were largely devoted to the study of 'modernity', to arrive at a prescription for replication for societies that were presumed to be non-modern.

Thus the pair of terms, 'modernity' and 'tradition', neither became tools of objective analysis nor indeed advanced our understanding of the actualities of social reality in different societies. They remained, by and large: encounter terms; superiority/inferiority (in all walks of life) terms; adulation/condemnation terms; trendsetter/emulator terms; in short, anything but that which encouraged critical inquiry into the complex social reality of developed as well as developing societies.

In a highly ambitious project on *Becoming Modern: Individual Change*

in Six Developing Countries, Alex Inkeles and David Smith got down
to the fundamentals of those attitudes and individual habits which
will help to sustain the complex requirements of an industrial
order.[16] In their way of thinking, such qualities have already been
developed by industrial societies and they have therefore registered
tremendous progress. Further, according to the authors, such qualities were confined to a few ethnic groups in some developing
countries. The authors, however, did not examine the extent of such
qualities in developed countries, in order to ensure that that is what
made the essential difference. As usual, such qualities, of attitude
and habit, were assumed to be universally present in people in developed countries. Nor did they examine the instances where, despite
strong attachment to 'traditional' values and social organisations,
a large number of individuals, in compartmentalised fashion, had
come up with as much industrial efficiency and 'modernity' in
specific areas as their counterparts in Western countries. This raised
the basic question as to how much 'modernity' was really needed
to be industrially efficient, a question which did not receive their
fullest attention. Finally, despite numerous traditional customs and
habits and, above all, communitarian values, the Japanese style of
industrialisation and management has become not only a threat but
a matter of envy and even emulation for Western countries.[17]

Inkeles and Smith, in their anxiety to prescribe a 'modernity'
exclusively of the Euro-american variety to traditional societies, overlooked the tremendous capacity of such societies to borrow and adjust
without totally giving up the traditional base of their social organisation. It is indeed difficult to think of a totally modernised (Wester-
nised) individual in non-Western societies.[18] The authors could not
get down to examining the actualities of the effective roles – corresponding to what a man or woman in industrial societies would
perform – of people in various walks of life in traditional societies
who remain deeply rooted in their cultural traditions and yet effectively, and with minimum conflict, perform their role in advancing
their societies both commercially and industrially.

The authors read too many negative qualities into their profile of
a 'non-modern' individual and too many positive qualities were
assumed by them in a 'modern' individual. At the root of such an
approach there was the basic flaw in conceiving individuals in exclusively 'modern' and 'non-modern' terms, as in the case of societies
in which they live, and leaving no room for permeation, adjustment
and coexistence and the contradiction of values with which an

individual can live. A large number of individuals in developing societies have functioned that way in industry, commerce, agriculture, education and the professions, and in legal and political institutions. The authors were therefore wide of the mark when they suggested that only 'modern' (Western) attitudes and habits, in their purity and entirety, can help sustain a 'modern' industrial economic order.

At the root of this there is the attempt to prescribe remedies and values to others that worked in one's own case, quietly assuming one's own superiority. Such an approach is often characterised by the awfully complex term: ethnocentrism. Ethnocentrism, unfortunately, has become a term of abuse and polemic. Rarely has it been used in order to indicate distortions in perceptions, evaluations and explanations caused by the unquestioned importance given to one's own values and then made available for universal prescription.

Ethnocentrism has been variously defined and interpreted. By and large it is considered to be 'an attitude or outlook in which values derived from one's own cultural background are applied to other cultural contexts where different values are operative'.[19] The most naive form of ethnocentrism takes its own values far too seriously, and often as the sole objective reality, and engages in passing judgements with reference to them on objects and events which are less familiar. A less pronounced ethnocentric position may formally take into account others' positions and cultural situations, but will nevertheless tend to characterise them as either inferior or not worthy of serious consideration.

One of the major thinkers to think through the problem of ethnocentrism – which originates in group encounters and results in characterisations in terms of 'we' and 'they', colouring the thinking of scholars and analysts – is Sumner. He brought together social, cultural, psychological and intellectual aspects of the phenomenon of ethnocentrism within a comparative framework. The pair of terms used by him to describe the units involved in an ethnocentric encounter was 'in group' and 'out group'. Accordingly, people within each 'in group' considered themselves to be at the centre of everything. They also considered themselves to be the standard-bearers of truth, right and worthiness. With the help of such sentiments, 'each group nourishes its own pride and vanity, boasts itself superior, exalts its own divinities, and looks with contempt at outsiders'.[20] Freud described ethnocentrism as 'a form of narcissism at the group level'.[21]

The concept of ethnocentrism, despite its crucial importance in comparative as well as development studies, has received scant attention. This is because the ramifications of the concept transcend the boundaries of several disciplines such as the social sciences, psychology, history, philosophy, theology, linguistics, etc. It aims at turning the cognitive process into a subject of inquiry. But apart from its unmanageability as a subject of inquiry, 'it strikes terror in the hearts of scholars', as Gabriel Almond put it, for their works of painstaking scholarship, and their well-meaning approach, could be branded as biased or distorted, with suspicion ranging from inevitable cultural bias, through scholarly neglect, to deliberate belittling and distortion. It is no wonder, therefore, that scholars do not like to delve deeply into this phenomenon.

While Inkeles and Smith stopped at the prescription of 'modernity' to the various developing countries which they studied, Daniel Lerner accused the countries of the Middle East of ethnocentrism for not adopting the modern ways so painfully developed by the countries of the West. In his words: 'A complication of Middle East modernisation is its own ethnocentrism – expressed politically in extreme nationalism, psychologically in passionate xenophobia.'[22]

Lerner believed passionately that liberal democratic institutions arise everywhere in an unmistakable sequence. Initially in the development of such institutions, 'Western men' had to go through 'titanic struggles' over centuries which included the great phases of human history, including the Age of Exploration, the Renaissance, the Reformation, the Counter Reformation, the Industrial Revolution, etc. Together they modernised the West industrially and politically. Since then the repetitive and unmistakable sequence is one of urbanisation, literacy, communication and competitive politics. Despite conflicts, tensions and distractions, the modernisation process is now reaching the average man in the Middle East and drawing him into the vortex of populist politics. Further, 'The model developed in the West is a historical fact . . . the same basic model reappears in virtually all modernising societies on all continents of the world, regardless of variations in race, colour, creed.'[23]

Lerner was not willing to examine the forces of history, culture and tradition which effectively make a difference to the reception of new political ideals and to the actual operations of public institutions which are either emulated or imposed. A careful examination of the countries of the Middle East and, in particular, Turkey, on which he concentrated, would have doubtless made him pay more attention to such forces. But to Lerner the receptivity and reinforcement, by indigenous institutions, of a political ideal emulated from outside, was unimportant. How much, for instance, the liberal democratic process in India has been reinforced by some of the cultural traditions and above all by the age-old participatory indigenous institution of *panchayat* (local council) is of no consequence to Lerner. He merely wanted country after country to join in the procession of modernisation, regardless of their background and problems.

III   REDUCTIONIST BIAS

The insensitivity to the peculiarity of different societies was not much in evidence in the writings of the founding fathers of functionalist theory, namely, Pareto and Radcliffe-Brown. Despite the built-in reductionist bias in their functionalist theories, which viewed societies as smooth functioning systems rather than ones which are incoherent amalgams of forces and processes, where order has to contend with chaotic contingency all the time, these two thinkers wanted to simplify only the differences *within* societies, not between them. While Pareto spoke of the need for the norms of society to be internalised by its members in order to guarantee its continuation, Radcliffe-Brown, the field-research social anthropologist, identified such a continuity, and its passing on to succeeding generations, by means of demonstrated patterns of behaviour of people in that society.

With Talcott Parsons, however, who introduced structural dimension to functionalist theory, two more factors were added. First of all he replaced the notion of internalisation with institutionalisation. For him a society, to be able to maintain itself, must have its value system institutionalised in its various institutions, goals and major roles. Mere internalisation of its values, he believed, would not guarantee their survival. Secondly, and more importantly, he introduced a highly oversimplified dichotomous theory of what he called 'pattern variables' by identifying different societies and their value systems as institutionalised in different compartments of their lives. For the purposes of classification, he provided pairs of polar opposite categories: traditional and modern; functionally-diffuse and functionally-specific; ascription-oriented and achievement-oriented; particularistic and universalistic, and so forth.

On the face of it, this exercise appeared to be an attempt, in the Weberian tradition, of making insightful theoretical statements which would illuminate the complexities of many behavioural and histor-

ical situations. But Weber guarded himself against its possible abuse
by providing the concept of 'ideal type'. Any 'ideal type' category,
Weber warned, does not exist in reality, but with its help, and with
a lot of qualifications and refinements, forced upon us by existential situations, one may be able to identify highly specific aspects of
social reality. Weber's 'ideal types', therefore, were not intended to
indicate their correspondence in social or historical reality, but as
initial conceptual tools in embarking on research, with qualifications,
refinements and reformulations of 'ideal types' to follow.

Parsonian 'pattern variables', on the other hand, had neither the
Weberian humility nor caution. Whatever qualifications Parsons
wanted to introduce remained blurred and incomprehensible as a
result of his excruciating writing style. To most social scientists, therefore, he appeared to have provided a series of concepts not for careful use and refinement but as ready-made classifications for
pigeon-holing various societies.

Once Parsons' 'pattern variables' were reduced to classificatory
categories, for living as well as historical societies, the function of
scholars was merely to pigeon-hole them under the polar opposite
labels that he provided. Under his reductionist dichotomous classification, societies either fell into the commendable category of being
modern, achievement-oriented, functionally-specific and universalistic or into the less desirable category of being traditional, ascription-
oriented, functionally-diffuse and particularistic. Such a rigid reductionist classification left little or no scope for moving out into the world
of social and political reality and discovering its complexities and
nuances, especially in the wide area between the two poles. And even
when attempts were made, at the level of research and analysis, the
very use of his conceptual vocabulary in one's writing, with all its
reductionist biases, made it extremely difficult to convey those social
and political actualities which defied his exclusive categories.

Parsonian reductionism vitally influenced Gabriel Almond and
through him, to some extent, Lucian Pye. Almond made a conscious
attempt to overcome the dichotomous Parsonian approach of classifying societies in opposing categories. Instead he introduced a
framework of comparative analysis which was supposed to be common to all societies regardless of their size, institutions or cultural
background. Apart from the reductionist biases involved in reduc-
ing everything to fit into a common framework, Almond never quite
escaped the reductionist biases of Parsonian conceptual vocabulary
which he freely used. And so far as Pye was concerned, he seemed

to accept the Parsonian reductionism of the two extremes, of modern and traditional societies. The modern societies of the West, for Pye, have set in motion the diffusion of ideas and influences through education, science, travel, etc. For him, as we shall see in the next section, such a diffusion of influence is a one-way process, from Western countries to non-Western countries, giving the former moral authority to judge what is wrong with the latter.

Almond's major, and highly influential work, *The Politics of the Developing Areas*, edited with James Coleman, expressed dissatisfaction with the 'conceptual vocabulary' of comparative government which, by and large, took political institutions into account. What he wanted instead was a group of concepts and categories which would help him identify 'political systems differing radically in scale, structure, and culture'.[24] For this purpose he was persuaded to look to sociological and anthropological theory. Of the two he took the prevailing sociological theory, presided over by the towering personality of Parsons, much more seriously. The Parsonian 'pattern variables' within a broad systemic approach of structural functionalism had an immense appeal for Almond. And what is more, they blended very well with his own comparative study of political systems within the framework of an input–output model.

In order to compare political societies *as* functioning political systems, he had to reduce them, first of all, to their systemic essentials. Such a system reduction put a premium on comparability, often at the expense of understanding the complex actualities of different societies. For the sake of systemic comparison, only those specific areas which were considered to be essential to the maintenance of various systems were taken into account. Then, within the functioning systems themselves, a second round of reduction followed. Almond did not want to compare different political societies merely from a systemic point of view but as comparable political systems within an input–output model. His model, therefore, imposed a further reduction of political systems into seven comparable units, on the two sides of his input–output divide. (Input functions: political socialisation and recruitment; interest articulation; interest aggregation; and political communication. Output functions: rule-making; rule-application; and rule adjudication.[25])

Finally, while Almond had some reservations about 'pattern variables', the Parsonian perspectives and concepts of polarised dichotomies remained very much at the centre of his comparative analysis. Almond too thus continued, at an intellectually less ambitious level, the tradition of understanding the complexities of the social and political life of emerging countries with the help of an untested speculative theory.

Almond did not take the problem of anthropological theory, and within it, that of comparative social anthropology, very seriously. In the 1950s, in particular, anthropology on both sides of the Atlantic was desperately trying to evolve theoretical frameworks so that the identification of the peculiarities of the non-Western societies did not suffer as a result of cognitive concepts and evaluative standards which were almost entirely rooted in Western social and cultural traditions. Consequently, without explicitly saying so, major anthropological works of that period often took different relativistic positions on societies that they examined.

Moreover, from the point of development studies, Almond was not attracted to the highly relevant universalistic–relativistic controversy in anthropology during the period in which he wrote on developing areas. From Almond's point of view, Parsons had already found a solution to that controversy in his 'pattern variables'. Consequently, instead of identification, analysis, description and explanation of the actualities of society and politics of developing countries, together with theoretical explorations into what makes them different from their Western counterparts, what his readers got was highly selective conceptual packaging for identifying the generalities of different societies in parallel terms.

Moreover, his use of certain concepts, deeply embedded in Western experience, brought into the framework of comparative analysis without qualifications or prior critical comments, further added to his reductionist biases. Comparison of different political systems was launched with the aid of concepts which were helpful in understanding a handful of Western countries. In use, however, such concepts either distorted the realities of other forms of political experience or failed to identify them and their peculiarities. Take, for instance, the following statement:

> Legitimate force is the thread that runs through the inputs and outputs of the political system, giving it its special quality and salience and its coherence as a system. The inputs into the political system are all in some way related to claims for the employment of legitimate compulsion . . . The outputs of the political system are also in some way related to legitimate physical compulsion . . . [26]

The above model of the use of legitimate force, which is largely based on Western democratic experience, was universalised in validity by Almond. In non-Western political systems, it is not the inputs which give legitimacy to the use of physical compulsion. That is only true of democratic systems where inputs are either electorally mandated or expressed through unfettered public opinion or indeed provided by means of legal and judicial discussions and decisions. In the developing countries, however, this has become the case only in a handful of countries where political authority is constituted by means of an electoral process within the framework of law and an independent judiciary. Nevertheless, in an overwhelming number of them legitimacy is *derived* from a baffling mixture of traditional factors ranging from the hereditary principle, religious sanctions, personal following, charisma, military support, cynical manipulation of power, and above all, being in charge of instruments of power. When confronted by a complex variety and degree of combination of such forces, one is inclined to question the adequacy of the concept of legitimacy itself in explaining non-Western non-democratic political experiences.

By not taking care of the concepts used, as in the case of legitimacy, Almond did himself a great disservice. For he either limited his own perception of the historical and behavioural complexities or vaguely accepted whatever filtered through such concepts, no matter how very limited or distorted, to get on with the predetermined exercise in comparability. Consequently, all the theoretically fashionable concepts of the period were used and used again without pausing to ask the crucial question whether they in fact enhanced the understanding of the actualities of societies, developed or developing.

Similarly, in the broader area of political development, Almond, instead of formulating new categories that were suitable to Western as well as non-Western societies, for the sake of *comparison*, depended heavily on the notion of 'modern' which is far too deeply grounded in the political experiences of a surprisingly small number of Western countries, and in the main Britain and the United States. In his words: 'The political scientist who wishes to study political modernisation in the non-Western areas will have to master the model of the modern, which in turn can only be derived from the most careful empirical and formal analysis of the functions of the modern Western polities.'[27]

By merely confining himself to the identification of parallels and deviants from an assumed and universally valid norm of 'political modernisation', Almond, and those who came under his influence, became insensitive to what happens to the actual operations of institutions and practices, which were borrowed from Western countries under a drive towards 'political modernisation', but are influenced and shaped by indigenous forces of culture and history. All that he and his associates wanted was to vindicate their claim to comparability of diverse societies with the help of their new conceptual tools, regardless of the fact that such comparability was of content-devoid formal parallels rather than of actuals.

The Civic Culture by Almond and Verba was another much discussed book on political development. This time Almond and his associate sought to bring within a common framework of comparison diverse countries such as Britain, the United States, Germany, Italy and Mexico. Since the standards of comparative judgement were entirely based on the Anglo-Saxon political experience, their externality to the countries such as Germany, Italy and Mexico was evident from the very start. Despite great care on the part of its authors, the sense of comparative caution, which is there in the writings of Max Weber, de Tocqueville and Reinhard Bendix, eluded them. Consequently in this work, instead of exploring the modern equivalent of the classical Greek notion of 'civic virtue', the authors assumed that, in a limited sense, it existed in Britain and the United States because these two countries were able to sustain their liberal political institutions for a greater length of time than others. They therefore sought to judge other political societies with the help of standards derived from the experiences of these two countries. The authors thus missed the unique opportunity of formulating the problem of comparative judgement in political development, a problem which could have initiated the much-needed discussion on the abstract universalistic standards for certain compartments of public life, and the context-dependent standards for the rest.

For Almond and Verba, since Britain and the United States, the two Anglo-Saxon countries, were able to sustain liberal institutions regardless of the quality of civic life in them, they became the embodiment of *civic culture*. What began as a search for civic virtue, in a classical Greek sense – in terms of principles applicable to a wide range of institutions and conditions – ended as rationalisations and elevations of existing shortcomings, compromises and adjustments that were typical of the politics of the two countries only. From them, their own limitations notwithstanding, was extrapolated a prescriptive norm of civic culture worthy of emulation everywhere. The 'givens' of Britain and the United States became the prescriptive ideals for other societies. The search for civic virtue was thus first of all reduced to civic culture and then civic culture itself was designated as constituting the necessary and sufficient condition for sustaining liberal political institutions as it did in those two countries. The social conditions which sustained liberal institutions in the countries of Scandinavia were of little consequence and therefore did not receive much attention. Nor was the question of how other countries, which did not have a civic culture, for complex historical reasons of their own, but would, nevertheless, strive towards it by means of their own trial and error process, of much interest to the authors. Civic culture thus became a matter of something which you either did or did not have; therefore, your political destiny, one way or the other, was sealed in advance of your endeavours.

What in fact sustained democratic institutions in Britain and the United States, assuming one can catalogue certain critical features common to them, may or may not be good enough for sustaining similar institutions in Germany, Italy and Mexico. Each of these countries has a very different background of culture and history and, therefore, would have required certain common as well as different conditions, suited to its background, to strive towards a civic culture that was typically suited to it. Such a difference exists between the respective civic cultures of Britain and the United States, despite a common historical legacy of political ideals and the growth of legal and political institutions.

What therefore had become indispensable for a comparative analysis of this nature is a commonly applicable notion of what, ideally speaking, civic culture ought to encompass, in abstract terms, on the one hand, and, given the different historical and cultural conditions of different countries, the unique component of each, on the other. That would then have taken care of the universal and particular aspects of the civic culture of each country.

But so great was the emphasis on equating the combined characteristics of British and American democracies, as constituting the very essence of the civic culture, that the authors missed the opportunity of developing vital arguments from one of their crucial assumptions – that 'the culture of the West is pluralistic'.[28] It was this assumption which remained in the background. Such a notion of culture could have helped the authors to develop the notion of plural democracies and many civic cultures. Instead of that, the overriding reductionist categories were brought in, by means of the rationalisation of the existing political practices in the two countries, and then elevated to the level of a universal principle of civic culture.

The authors conceded the fact that there are different 'mixes' in the political cultures of different countries; within different countries there are different proportions of 'mixes' of the parochial, the subject and the participant in their political cultures. Nevertheless, so far as Britain and the United States were concerned, the 'mixes' of these three were in the right proportion. How else would they have succeeded in sustaining democracy? Even the political passivity within their political culture, according to the authors, is of the right proportion. Too much political participation would have made their respective democracies unworkable.[29]

The Civic Culture, thus, with all its painstaking research in five countries of the world, missed the opportunity of becoming a work which could have exercised a paradigmatic influence on the course of the study of political development. The pity of it was that it came so close to doing it. For it recognised the plurality of political societies, and the 'mixes' of political cultures within all of them. Moreover, it had the opportunity to give a valuable message to the emerging countries of our time, with different cultures and traditions of their own, about what can be learnt with regard to civic culture, by examining the trial and error process, and the incremental political learning of the developed countries themselves. That, indeed, was the emphasis of Almond's teacher, Charles Merriam, and also of the thinkers of classical Greece who dared to talk about what in fact should be done to attain civic virtue. Instead what we have in this book is an attempt at the self-idealisation and exclusivity of a civic culture club.

The implicit reductionist bias, this time, lay in ignoring the political experiences of the countries of the Old Commonwealth, Scandinavia and of the New Commonwealth, in particular India and Sri Lanka. In any general definition of civic culture, which the authors attempted, their experiences were of as much significance as those of Britain and the United States. For in some of them we see not only the adaptations of borrowed legal and political institutions to different cultural conditions, but also attempts at resilience after constant infractions against them. The drama of their effort at evolving civic culture is taking place before our very eyes.

After the publication of *The Civic Culture*, Sidney Verba, by means of his highly rigorous empirical approach, emerged as a major scholar in the comparative field. Instead of comparing the democratic components of different societies, he zeroed in on specific areas such as equality and participation in them and produced works of great rigour and soundness.

Subsequently, Almond, along with Bingam Powell, made a serious attempt in their *Comparative Government: A Developmental Approach* to 'break out of parochialism and ethnocentrism'.[30] Unfortunately, there too they could not avoid their reductionist bias reinforcing what they wanted to get away from. Their inability to think in terms of a conceptual language applicable to a wider range of political experiences blocked their escape routes from parochialism and ethnocentrism from the very start. Consequently, neither in their comparative analysis, nor in their comparative judgement, could they go beyond the norms of relevance and judgement that were rooted in the Anglo-Saxon political experience.

The book was written with the avowed aim of helping teachers who deal with Western as well as non-Western countries with a common comparative framework, and of reviving the 'classic' relationships between comparative government and political theory in the treatment of various themes.[31] For Almond, in particular, the aim of the book provided an opportunity to enter into the 'applied' field of how to approach the problem of comparative politics with the help of ideas that he had already developed in the two major works of his which we have discussed so far.

Almond rightly described the post Second World War situation, with so many emerging countries with their own cultural background wanting to establish new political institutions, as requiring a different kind of approach in comparative studies. But by that time his own group of like-minded scholars, which had produced impressive studies on several developing countries, had also emerged as an exclusive group, with little or no intellectual contact with scholars holding different views, and with all the psychological preparations to launch a new orthodoxy.

What was indeed baffling in the scholarly enterprise of this group was its inability to learn from the very valuable experiences of social anthropologists who, by now, had nearly 100 years of experience of field research in non-Western societies. Even the distinguished sociologist, Edward Shils, with his many insightful writings on non-Western countries, had a limited influence on the group.

From 1954, when Almond was appointed to the chairmanship of the Committee on Comparative Government, to the 1970s, his main concern was how to develop a *common* theoretical framework for the study of different political societies. But at no stage was there a discussion on what such a framework would involve by way of prior work. The isolated responsibility of understanding different societies was left to scholars working in different developing countries. Nevertheless, a curious and self-defeating routine was followed, particularly in the relationship between the individual scholar and the chairman of the committee, namely Almond, who remained in charge of the overall direction of several projects. While the individual scholar reported to the chairman on his findings, the chairman himself provided the individual scholar with a theoretical framework *in advance* of his actual field research. Consequently, the individual scholar, working in an unfamiliar developing country, with little or no facility for the local language, had no alternative but to 'validate' such a theoretical framework given to him in advance of his research operations. In the various publications which followed, there is little or no evidence of individual scholars saying how they were forced to refine or reconstruct earlier theoretical presuppositions in the light of what they actually saw or understood on the spot.

Such a division of work, with Almond in charge of theoretical direction and the various regional experts in charge of collecting empirical material, did not help Almond very much either. Almond's own theoretical formulations remained almost unaltered by the group's findings, and therefore untested as to their capacity either to illuminate the complexities of the phenomenon or to explain what was observed in coherent terms. In rigidly, and not tentatively, presenting his theoretical position, in advance of actual field research, Almond lost the valuable opportunity of refining his theoretical formulations in the post-research period. To him, therefore, the reductionist correspondence between the assumptions implicit in his theoretical formulations, on the one hand, and the complex social and political reality of the developing countries, on the other, was never in doubt. Once he had formulated his theory, he knew what there was to know. The empirical and 'validating' research which followed provided only the second proof of the correctness of the theoretical position already advanced.

Almond was even forced to guess about the social and political realities of the developing countries before he could actually visit some of them. Only several years after he became the chairman of one of the most ambitious academic programmes was he able to visit some of the developing countries. And curiously enough, only two years *after* he published his *Politics of the Developing Areas* (1960) was he able to make an extended visit to developing countries. In his words: 'I was given the unusual opportunity, in 1962–63, to spend a year in Japan, Southeast Asia, India, and Africa. This was my first direct and sustained exposure to non-European cultures . . .'[32]

Had he visited these countries before his research programme was finalised, there is every likelihood that a theoretical approach would have emerged which would not have taken the correspondence between its own assumptions and the social and political reality of the developing countries for granted. It would have left it to field research to determine and, if necessary, refine it.

Thus Almond, with the best of intentions, could not get round to questioning the reductionist and distorting effects of his own conceptual tools of analysis. Such conceptual tools were too much a part of his cognitive process to become objects of inquiry or self-inquiry. Moreover, the intellectual isolation and close-mindedness of the group he founded was of little help. It neither brooked criticism nor engaged in a dialogue with scholars who had a few critical things to say. What was worse, it shrugged off the criticisms of scholars from developing countries whose societies the group had claimed to study. Invariably scholars from underdeveloped countries were either presumed to have underdeveloped minds or fit only to become research contractors, supervising data collection on the group's behalf.

A curious kind of 'science' was being developed, where the voices of criticism were excluded from the very start. The impressive list of publications, in succession, in major publishing houses of the world, created a false sense of intellectual security and correctness of theoretical direction. By the late 1970s the group ran out of steam and no one in it wanted to consider another lease of life for it.

IV   DIFFUSIONIST BIAS

In a major study of Burma published under the title of *Politics, Personality, and Nation-Building*, Lucian Pye adopted a psychological as well as a diffusionist approach to study a society in transition. He rightly identified the tremendous psychological impact of colonialism and the consequent national movement on the people of Burma as a whole. Coupled with that was the diffusion or the spread of 'the world culture', which had originated in the West but by means of education, travel, science and technology had spread to the different parts of the world. So colonialism, nationalism and diffusionism (modernisation – Westernisation) had, together, created, according

to Pye, immense *psychological* problems for the people of Burma. So
great were the psychological problems for the people caught in the
vortex of modernisation that they were often afraid to try out new
ideas either because of their novelty or because of the 'fear of failure' in trying them. Such a reaction on a massive scale created 'psychological inhibitions to effective action'. The student of emerging
societies must, therefore, clearly understand, Pye argued, the immen-
sity of the psychological problems of the people of those societies.
In Pye's words: 'The shocking fact has been that in the last decade
the new countries of Asia have had more difficulties with the psychological than with the objective economic problems basic to
nation-building.'[33]

Again, 'it is a tragedy of transitional society that the processes of
change create profound insecurities in its people which cause them
to feel a deep need to be bound to others, to escape the sense of
individual isolation'.[34]

The picture which Pye had in mind seems to be one of urbanisation in Western society or of migration of surplus labour from the
rural south to the industrial north in the United States. In the
developing countries of Asia to which Pye refers, modernisation has
been a process of building upon the traditional layer of society which
is already there. It is unrealistic to think that any society, in its process of modernisation, would become totally unhinged from its traditional base, dissolving all its existing social ties, and creating a total
sense of isolation and insecurity in its people. The reason for considering such a possibility arises because the very process of modernisation is erroneously conceived in exclusively puristic terms of
expunging all the vestiges of traditional group living and acting.

In the traditional societies of Asia, 'change' has meant a total abro-
gation neither of the existing cultural life nor of social relationships.
A change from a system of barter to monetised economy, compul-
sory education for children, modern means of transport, use of new
seeds and fertilisers, modern medicine, artificial insemination of
milch animals, visits to family planning clinics, and above all, constitution of political authority on the basis of one man one vote have
together created a number of problems and conflicts, but hardly any,
as field researchers in rural and urban Asia would point out, which
imposed an unbearable sense of individual isolation or drove people
out of their wits.

In the rural district of Mehsana, in Gujarat, Western India, in
the late 1970s, crossbred cows were displacing buffaloes, which have

been the milch animal in the area for centuries. The crossbreeding was done by means of frozen semen artificially injected into the local and very nearly discarded cows. The villagers, and particularly the women, often noted the code numbers of the frozen semen tube, waited for the results in terms of milk yield of the female calves, and four or five years later asked the vets, after making a comparative evaluation of milk yields of each, for that specific frozen semen which produced the best results. All this took place in a form of traditional social and economic life which, at least outwardly, had not changed for centuries. And still major changes were being assimilated with minimum disruptions.

The people of traditional societies often worked out a place for the new values, in most compartments of their lives, within their highly accommodating and assimilating social structures.[35] The most uncomfortable people in all this were the old venerated men, religious and caste leaders and people with high familial status.

Intensive research needs to be done precisely in this field which can tell us more about the adjustment and incorporation processes, with instances of disruption identified rather than inferred, in traditional societies when they are exposed to modernisation in various compartments of life. One of the distorting perspectives, in the understanding of that process, is the diffusionist theory. To that we now turn.

Several versions of diffusionist theory gained currency in Europe and North America by the turn of this century. Its main argument was commonsensical. It implied that any powerful or worthwhile culture and its various components spread from the place of its origin to surrounding areas. It also implied that there are various *Kulturkreise* or culture circles which are either concentrated or dispersed in different geographical areas.[36] Such a formulation immediately gave rise to the notions of culture areas and culture centres.

Soon another concept opposed to diffusion, namely, independent invention, rather than exposure to outside influence, hit the scene. In the controversy which ensued, both of them began to lose their following. For one thing, the controversy dichotomised the nature of cultural influence without intensively examining specific areas in order to advance our understanding of the actualities of such an influence. The greatest critic of the controversy between diffusion and independent invention, as also of unilinear evolutionism, was Franz Boas. He argued that it was erroneous to attribute a grand system of uniform evolutionism, through diffusion or otherwise, to different cultural manifestations. In his words:

> we must . . . consider all ingenious attempts at construction of
> a grand system of the evolution of society as of very doubtful
> value, unless at the same time proof is given that the same
> phenomenon must always have had the same origin. Unless this
> is done, the presumption is always in favour of a variety of courses
> which historical growth may have taken.[37]

Boas was a strong supporter of historical particularism and, after
him, at least in anthropological theory, there were not many instances
where a grand diffusionist movement was seen as wiping out the
traditional bases of different social organisations.

In political development, however, the exposure to the Western
state system – with its legal, governmental and public institutions
– was seen by some scholars, and in particular by Lerner and Pye,
as a powerful diffusionist force which could alter the political arrangements of traditional societies and modernise them, economically and
politically, almost on the lines of Western societies.

While building a case-study of Burma to illustrate his diffusionist
approach, Pye in the preface to his book warned his readers, and
also cautioned himself, by saying that 'the Burmese case is not so
rudely forced into the model that it is stripped of all the flavourful
eccentricities that make it unique'.[38]

But in order to unravel the cause and consequence of Burma's psychological crisis, Pye's own caution gave way and he began to see
Burma's relentless modernisation stripping her people of the cushion
of security provided by her traditional society. The deep psychological
problems of her people, of individual isolation and insecurity, are
likely to continue, in his view, as long as they are in a state of transition from traditional to modern (Western). In such a transition,
colonialism and nationalism provided only a part of the answer to

> the process of change, of acculturation and transformation in
> which both whole societies and individual personalities are forced
> to take new forms. A shorthand label for this complex process
> could be the diffusion of the western culture: a culture which
> represents the essence of much of the culture of the West, its place
> of origin, but which no longer has clear geographic boundaries;
> a culture composed of such basic concepts and practices as the
> secular state and the industrialised organisation of human activi-

ties, the reliance upon rational and conscious choice and a faith in impartial justice, and the acceptance of the virtue of merit and of rewards according to skill.[39]

Pye has attributed much greater force, for rapid social change, to Western modernistic diffusion in non-Western societies than in fact has been the case. Despite Western education, deep commitment to Western social and political values on the part of thinking men and women, and above all large-scale and sometimes overenthusiastic and indiscriminate emulation of its legal and political institutions in the traditional societies, neither their indigenous values nor social and cultural institutions have totally disappeared. In most cases they have made their own adjustments and accommodations with what has come from outside. In most cases, again, even the very operations of the transplanted institutions have acquired different characteristics as a result of the deeper roots, and greater adjustability, of traditional values and social organisations than the diffusionists would have us believe.

Traditional societies are not like containers from which you throw out old contents and fill them with new. They are more like the multi-layered earth where the lower layers do not disappear. They stay there and continue to influence the life that goes on above them, for an unlimited span of time.

Students of political development have paid heavily for their neglect of the durability and the subtle influence of the traditional bases of all societies. Such bases exercise no less an influence on industrialised societies. Their neglect has led to an oversimplified view of the actualities of political development as such, not only in developing societies but also in developed ones. In the next three chapters we shall point out how, in searching for the parallels of political development, parallel to the assumed standard course set by a few Western political societies, we often fail to understand the complexities of the actual course of their development.

V ANTHROPOLOGISTS AND THE PROBLEM OF WESTERN BIAS

Social anthropologists, British, American and French, after an initial period of avoidance, faced the basic problem of the Western bias forthrightly while studying non-Western societies. The problem had continued to plague them even when they gave up thinking of non-Western people as: 'primitive societies'; having no sense of shame (John Lubbock); 'pre-logical' (Lévy-Bruhl); or just an 'inferior version of ourselves'. Their scholarly conscience, together with lively criticism of each other's works, unlike in political development studies, kept the search for a satisfactory approach to non-Western societies alive for more than a century. Some of the major perspectives which emerged from controversies among them were as follows: to view non-Western societies as eventually following the route which Western societies took; to look for the disappearance of their traditional cohesion in their encounter with exploitative colonial rule which will then put them on the way to European-style class conflict (Marx); to look for their continued social cohesion as the same did not disappear in industrial societies (Durkheim); to discover structural–functional equivalents of their social practices similar to those in modern societies; and to build a judgement-free, relativistic science which embraces all societies (the bulk of social anthropologists).

Then there was the problem of reverse bias, of viewing industrially developed societies, if you are a social anthropologist, in terms of the non-Western society that you had studied. It was relatively easier to submit oneself to the scholarly community for one's biases in studying non-Western societies than to put up with accusations of the reverse bias. Practically all the distinguished anthropologists, after their major bouts of field research in developing countries, were accused of such a bias.[40]

It is difficult to think of a scholar without his conscious or semiconscious bias, implicit in his approach, model, choice of theories and concepts, or cultural background in general. Moreover, the cognitive process involved in research of societies other than one's own is not conducted with a blank mind. Biases, in short, influence all our acts of knowing. It is our awareness of biases, and constant scrutiny of them by the scholarly community to which we belong, that help us to realise and emphasise the essentially relational character of our knowledge. Such a *social* character of knowing also reminds us, from time to time, of the extent to which the results of our cognitive process get undermined, exaggerated, distorted, coloured or specially selected by our own biases.[41] The integral part of knowing, then, is the scholarly community and the society as a whole, where knowledge is communicated and used either for intellectual or applied policy purposes.

Social anthropologists, very early in the development of their science of society, sensitised their fellow scholars to the problem of bias and the need for constant scholarly scrutiny of their works. An opposite course was followed by the subdiscipline of political development which, like social anthropology, was also engaged in studying non-Western societies. The former, i.e. political development, encouraged a collective orthodoxy in intellectual approaches and looked with disapproval at a very limited number of criticisms which began to appear. Consequently, like other intellectual orthodoxies before it, it very nearly dried up the sources of its own continued dynamism.

Over and above the problem of cultural bias, the social anthropologists were also concerned with the bias implicit in the tools of theoretical analysis, i.e. speculative theory preceding field research; theory-directed field research; and theory-oriented field research reportage. Since most of these theories were either rooted in the social and political experiences of Western countries, or were developed at the conclusion of one's field research in non-Western societies to become an integral part of the body of mainstream theoretical knowledge which was growing in Western countries, the problem of bias, in that respect, was in fact a twofold problem. Although unresolved as a problem of what to do with the biases in theoretical approaches, the variety of controversy relating to that central question is highly illuminating. To that we now turn.

Montesquieu, in his *The Spirit of the Laws* (1748), spoke of the possibility of discovering 'laws' to which human relations – in religious matters, economy, social dealings and political conduct in general – conform.[42] For him, the question was whether one can identify such relations in terms of theories and, better still, laws. Montesquieu's inspiration of weaving theories and laws into one's understanding of human social relationships has been an abiding force in social anthropology and keeps reappearing at different times in the writings of different thinkers.

At the other extreme the field research anthropologists, as opposed to pure theorists, start off with the initial determination to be theory-free, and to learn about the actualities of social life of various communities so as not to let the biases implicit in theory distort one's field research understanding. But they, too, either in their search for developing a comparative perspective, or in subscribing to a widely-held structural–functional approach, or indeed in reporting their findings in terms of mainstream theoretical knowledge, end up by

sharing its biases. In the following pages we shall identify their efforts
to mirror social reality, as truthfully as possible, and examine how
they finally seek recourse, some more consciously than others, in a
variety of cultural relativism.

The first group of crude field researchers were the colonial adminis-
trators and missionaries.[13] They began collecting information on
cultural institutions of the people of colonies in order to make their
own work among them more effective. They produced gazetteers,
monographs, diaries, autobiographical accounts, etc., in which some
effort, however tendentious, was made to *understand* different people
rather than to condemn them as heathens and savages. Then began
an impressive effort at field research on the part of anthropologists,
on both sides of the Atlantic, which revolutionalised the nature of
anthropology. Some of the major contributors to this were Franz Boas
and Morgan in the United States, and Malinowski, Radcliffe-Brown
and Evans-Prichard in Britain. Among these, the influence of Boas
and Malinowski on a generation of students, and especially on their
perspectives on the non-Western world, was profound.

Boas, in particular, consciously avoided the implicit bias of theory
in whatever he studied and therefore became a stickler for what was
dubbed as 'inductive purity'.[44] Subsequently, historians of anthropology, and his own critics, saw in his theory-free approach the theory of historical particularism. Malinowski equally emphatically
emphasised the supreme importance of what was observed as opposed
to what was inferred from it.[45] But their caution did not go very far
with their students and, once again, theory, with all its problems,
reemerged as preeminent in anthropology.

In Britain two major anthropologists, namely, Evans-Prichard and
Radcliffe-Brown, tried cautiously to balance empirical field research
in non-Western societies with Western theory. Evans-Prichard, in particular, claimed that anthropology, being a relatively young social
science, had not developed its own 'technical vocabulary' and was,
therefore, forced to borrow terms such as 'society', 'culture', 'custom',
'religion', 'sanction', 'structure', 'function', etc. It had to do this before
its own requisite tools of conceptual analysis evolved. His preference,
however, was for commonly used language as opposed to the 'obscu-
rities' and presuppositions of 'specialist jargon'.[46]

Despite their enormous emphasis on field research, the British
anthropologists were deeply attracted to the idea of building 'a positive science of society' as envisaged by Montesquieu and rationalist
anthropologists such as Durkheim and Lévy-Bruhl. Nearer home,

the ideas of Adam Smith and David Hume – suggesting that 'societies are natural systems' and outgrowths of human nature rather than products of artificial social contract, and that along with one's research one should be able to identify, rationally, the dimensions of such a system – also had their own attraction for anthropologists. Such ideas, however, made a much greater impression on Radcliffe-Brown than on Evans-Prichard.

Radcliffe-Brown sought to bring about a major shift in British social anthropology. For him it was not enough to identify and report observed particulars of social life by means of one's field research; one had also to identify the social system within which they functioned in a related and coherent fashion.[47]

Evans-Prichard, however, leaned more towards the knowing of specific systems within different cultures rather than inferring them as parallels of what was suggested by Western experience. Thus in his writings Evans-Prichard moved more and more towards a position of cultural relativism. In his *Witchcraft, Oracles, and Magic Among the Azande*, in particular, he had argued that we might show a cultural bias if we tried to understand the practice of magic among the Azande as a rival of religion. For that would be tantamount to understanding such a practice with the help of a highly generalised theory of religion of our own.[48]

A similar emphasis on cultural relativism was very much in evidence in the writings of Boas. As we noted earlier, he was one of the strongest critics of the tendency to view different cultural organisations either within the framework of a cultural unilinear evolution or a grand theory.

In social anthropology one of the strongest criticisms of distortions caused by one's concepts and theories, and in particular by the theory of structural–functionalism, came from Gregory Bateson, the author of *Naven* (1936). He studied anthropology under Radcliffe-Brown. After paying a tribute to Radcliffe-Brown, for having taught him how to look at a cultural phenomenon in an integrated fashion, Bateson complained that the same phenomenon looked different when viewed from the perspectives of structuralism and functionalism, separately. In his words, 'each of our separate methods involves distortions and gives but a partial view of the phenomenon'.[49] Implied in his critique were the nightmarish questions as to how you either select one perspective over another, or put together findings obtained through two different perspectives, or be sure that through the use of each perspective you have not distorted your understanding of the phenomenon itself.

As in other disciplines, anthropological research goes on within the framework of the existing body of theoretical ideas and their questioning and refining at the end of each scholar's field research. But as a branch of the social sciences, devoted to intensive field research on highly specific themes and areas, and in particular in the non-Western world, it often reports its dissatisfaction with the way in which our concepts and theories distort our understanding of the social reality of that part of the world. In a fascinating paper, Robin Horton quoted a review of M. Fortes's *The Web of Kinship Among the Tallensi* where the reviewer had difficulty in seeing the relationship or boundary between the abstract anthropological concepts of the Cambridge school and the cultural practices of a tribe in Africa or, indeed, the relationship between a group of hefty Parsonian concepts and the day-to-day life of an agricultural community in the non-Western world.[50]

Students of political development have much to learn from the controversies and hesitations of anthropologists who, like themselves, examine specific aspects of human behaviour and the operations of social and political institutions in situations which are deeply influenced by different cultures – and do not indiscriminately assume, or press for, the universal validity of their theoretical knowledge, which is often based on the limited experiences of a few countries. The agonising and interminable controversy among anthropologists on relativism ought to induce students of political development to take a hard look at their own concepts and theories and their distorting effect on their own understanding of the non-Western world.

The various biases identified in this chapter are in a sense necessary stages in our learning and correcting process. They are similar to the initial stages of scientific knowledge in any discipline where scholars go from familiar to unfamiliar fields by exploring the validity of their knowledge from one field to another. Nevertheless, after their initial explorations, if they fail to examine doubts and criticisms of the validity and adequacy of their approaches, they then cease to pursue dependable or worthwhile knowledge.

In the study of political development, then, what has been sorely lacking is the need to pay attention to the post-exploratory stage where doubts and criticisms of various theoretical approaches have been expressed. At the centre of such criticisms is the view that because of various biases, which in turn generated distorted perspectives on the non-Western world, we have failed to grasp the extent of diversity among various political societies and the actuality of their development processes. In the following pages we shall examine some of the instances of such diversity, emphasising the need to cultivate sensitivity to the actual operations of social and political institutions and the quality of public life which they provide.

2 Diversity and Actuality of Political Societies

In the previous chapter we identified the broad framework of assumed universals of political development within which certain biases operate. Such biases, as we pointed out, prevent us from identifying and understanding the diversity and actuality of the processes of development of different political societies. Despite the exposure of the political elite of developing countries to the political ideals and institutions of Western countries, and despite their earnest attempts to transplant some of them in their own societies in the post-colonial period, the actual operations of such institutions, and the quality of public life which they provide, are vitally influenced by their own history, tradition and culture. Moreover, such transplants, and their underlying normative emphases, interact with indigenous institutions and practices and what they consider to be normatively desirable. Together, these give rise to a complex political diversity in different political societies. Such a diversity and the actuality of the development process within each society, needs to be identified and understood and not ignored for the sake of validating any particular universal theory.

Apart from considering the post-colonial borrowings as an unmixed import, what has also prevented us from recognising political diversity is the lack of sensitivity to it in the corpus of our theoretical knowledge. Such a corpus, as Reinhard Bendix has pointed out, originated in a handful of Western countries, and deeply assimilated the social and political experiences of those countries, to the exclusion of the experiences of other countries.[1] Furthermore, there is the widespread practice among most scholars of going through the ritual of formal expression of dissatisfaction with theoretical knowledge and, having done that, returning to the practice of using such knowledge without qualifications.

But there have also been a few attempts to explain why despite common exposure and parallel attempts at transplanting legal and political institutions, different political societies manifested a different quality of public life. We shall illustrate this claim with the help of brief references to certain political societies of Asia, Africa and Latin America. Their diversity, in fact, constitutes a living challenge to our corpus of theoretical knowledge in political development which is premised on the assumption that the diffusion of Western political ideals and institutions will result in the creation of a corresponding social and political situation in developing countries. And if they fail to create or evolve a parallel social and political condition then either they are deviants or in the state of inferior being. We shall, however, argue that such assumptions are misplaced: what we need instead is an approach which helps us to understand political diversity and its nuances. By recognising their diversity, to begin with, we shall be able to think in terms of their quintessential unity – in certain basic matters to be able to judge the quality of their public life – rather than insist on the replication of a Western prototype as the ultimate achievement. This chapter is divided into the following parts: (i) some theories of social change; (ii) thinkers who emphasised the need to recognise political diversity; and (iii) the political actuality of some of the non-Western countries of South Asia, Africa, the Middle East and Latin America. We shall now examine each of them in some detail.

I SOME THEORIES OF SOCIAL CHANGE

A number of scholars who have written on the theory of social change in recent years have expressed dissatisfaction with the assumed universals of social and political development in our perspectives on different societies. Such scholars objected, in particular, to the notion of unilinear evolution, which is entirely grounded in the experiences of a few Western societies, as an inevitable course of development for other societies. However, despite questioning the notion of a corresponding evolution of non-Western societies, they failed to guard against the fallacy of the dichotomous notion of tradition and modernity, which they thought would provide an alternative to universal evolutionism. This is because the different versions of the tradition–modernity theory directly or indirectly reaffirmed the unilinear assumptions of evolutionary theory.

Comte's vision of the inevitability of the evolution of civilisation; Maine's emphasis on the state rather than the family as the principal object of loyalty under the influence of Roman Law and, consequently, a revolution in human relationship, from status to contract; Toennis's identification of the *Gemeinschaft* of rural life as being replaced by the *Gesellschaft* of sprawling urban life; Spencer's and Durkheim's beliefs in specialisation, differentiation and integration – all of these almost entirely derived from European experiences – became core issues not only of evolutionary theorists but also, after them, of modernisation theorists in their explanations of social change and development in the non-Western world. To these were added the views of Levy,[2] on the shift from animate to inanimate power, and the views on rationality, rigidly extrapolated from the life-style of the Western urban dweller, by Inkeles.[3]

The bulk of scholars who have studied social change in the non-Western world have been from the Western countries. And not all of them review critically their own perspectives, emphases and the adequacy of their conceptual tools as often as is needed. Despite an increasingly nagging feeling of uneasiness among them as to the validity of their interpretations, very rarely do they themselves engage in the reformulation of their own approaches. For the bulk of them, therefore, despite their persistent doubts, it has become a routine exercise in extending the use of knowledge from a familiar Western field to a much less familiar non-Western field. To others it has become an exercise in validating grand theories formulated much in advance of sufficient understanding of the areas they are supposed to explain.

Until the rise of industrial capitalism – accompanied by the development of urban civilisation, experimental and applied science, the modern state and its bureaucratic apparatus, and what Max Weber called 'rational laws' – the social and economic development of Western countries had been gradual. Most of those countries took 200 to 300 years to attain the level of development that was in evidence in the nineteenth century. And most of the gradual changes which took place in those societies were largely the products of the interaction of social and economic forces. Rarely was the conscious choice of the political elite able to force the pace of change in those countries.

The corpus of theoretical knowledge which sought to explain such an experience of Western countries, therefore, heavily underlined the importance of *objective* historical forces in bringing about social change. Simultaneously, it played down the importance of the individual, barring a few exceptions, in being able to play a crucial role in the face of the forces of history. Such a diminished individual role is implicit in the ideas of such diverse thinkers as Comte, Marx and Spencer. For them, human intervention in creating specific social situations was inconsequential.[4]

As opposed to the gradual social and economic development of the countries of the West, the non-Western countries, ever since their emergence, have been trying to force the pace of change despite a backlog of problems. In doing so, they are engaged in what is appropriately termed 'century-skipping'. In deciding to accelerate the pace of change, their political elites have played a vital role. In their economic planning, in setting up social and political institutions, in bringing about legal, administrative and educational reforms, they did not wait for the forces of history to tell them what to do. They, on the other hand, consciously made choices and decisions, of far-reaching importance, mobilised their human and material resources in support of them, and swiftly acted on whatever they had decided to do. In their cases, therefore, there was the plurality of elite-made choices together with a diversity of social and political consequences resulting from such choices.

Moreover, most of the developing countries made their choices, which reflected a conscious desire on their part to transplant Western public institutions, together with education, science, technology, medicine, etc., *within* the framework of their cultural heritage. The crucial diversity of initial choices, together with the highly complex diversity resulting from the interaction between the indigenous and the borrowed institutions and their norms, which has been different in different cases, is often missed out by those theorists of social change who want to see everything in universal terms.

Furthermore, modernisation, or what is emulated from the West, is often seen by the theorists of social change in terms of *block* borrowing rather than select borrowing. Consequently, according to this view of borrowing, the borrower must look, operate and behave in essential matters like those it borrowed from. The phenomenon of select borrowing, and the diversity resulting therefrom, as well as from the interaction of the indigenous and the borrowed, was either not understood or played down by modernisation theorists.[5]

Another fruitless emphasis on the part of modernisation theorists has been on what is vaguely referred to as 'cultural integration'. Under this category, the incompatibility and contradiction between the indigenous and the borrowed is highly exaggerated to the point of unliveability. Instead of identifying the actuality of coexistence, interpenetration and social change resulting from the interaction of the indigenous and the borrowed, the modernisation theorists often picture relentless victory for their own forces working towards integration. Integration thus becomes just another term for replicating what exists in the West.

In most plural societies, developed or developing, diverse ethnic, religious and racial groups coexist with strong cultural differences and identities. In other societies, which are culturally less differentiated, class and regional differences may coexist. Still there are others in which cultural diversity rises or declines as a result of migrations at different stages in their history. In all these what needs to be noted is that practically all societies may have certain cultural, behavioural, attitudinal differences and incompatibilities within themselves. But despite such differences and incompatibilities, different groups learn to coexist, transact their business with each other in essential matters, air grievances and express their indifference in other matters. Very few societies attain 'cultural integration'. What they do attain, however, is the sharing of notions of decency, propriety, legitimacy, justice, freedom, standard of living, quality of public life, etc., together with commonly supported institutions to realise them.

Apart from the underlying assumptions of the theories of unilinear evolutionism, and their heir, modernism, what has prevented the identification and analysis of the diversity of social and political phenomena, in non-derogatory terms, is the manner in which they are perceived. Anything that is different from a self-possessed model has to be viewed in terms of its parallels. And if it goes beyond the notions of 'sameness' with a difference or parallel, it is then branded as 'deviant', and its characteristics of inferiority are then identified. What is different is then perceived either as a product of resistance to the forces of change, with an underlying assumption that change must produce similar results everywhere, or as a 'fragment' which has lost its original dynamic because of its extraction or transfer from the source.[6]

Robert Nisbet thus identified, in value terms, the polarity of tradition and modernity, respectively, as follows: 'hierarchy, community, . . . authority, and the sacred', on the one hand, and 'egalitarianism, individualism, secularism, and power', on the other.[7] In making such a discrete dichotomy between the values of tradition (indigenous) and modernity (borrowed), Nisbet ruled out in advance their shades of coexistence and mixture in all societies, developed or developing.

In his subsequent writings, Nisbet viewed the phenomenon of

change, not from the position of the dichotomy of tradition and modernity, but from the perspectives of 'structure' as suggested by Radcliffe-Brown and 'paradigm' as suggested by Thomas Kuhn. For Radcliffe-Brown it was important to make a distinction between change within the structure and change of the structure itself. A similar distinction was made by Kuhn in his notions of normal science and extraordinary science.

Such a perspective helped Nisbet to appreciate Max Weber's rejection of the 'fallacy of emanationism'. Max Weber in his writings on the rise of capitalism had argued that the capitalist form of social and political organisation had not merely emanated from feudalism but in a genuine sense was something new and different. In making capitalism what it was, a large number of social, economic, religious and cultural forces had converged in the most effective manner.

Despite broadly subscribing to Weber's rejection of the fallacy of emanationism, Nisbet failed to question the emanation bias implicit in the tradition–modernity dichotomy, which made the developing countries either emanated progenies of their traditional past or emanated replicates of modernised Western societies.

The borrowing from the West by the developing countries, and the grafting, have been highly selective. In a selective fashion, they have absorbed from developed countries in areas which they think are useful or exciting. Whatever they absorbed, they grafted on to the indigenous, and in the course of time tried to indigenise whatever was borrowed. In that process they have themselves begun to change from their pre-borrowing position – without cloning or replicating where they had borrowed from, no matter how much they admired it – to whatever the interaction between the indigenous and the borrowed made them. Such an interaction has contributed to the diversity of political development. But before we examine some of the examples of such diversity, let us briefly consider the ideas of a few scholars who have sensitised us to the need to recognise, initially, beyond the laudatory–condemnatory framework, the very presence of such a diversity.

II THINKERS WHO EMPHASISED THE NEED TO RECOGNISE POLITICAL DIVERSITY

These thinkers were, among others, de Tocqueville, Max Weber, Veblen, Schumpeter and Bendix. Together they provided a wide range of arguments supporting the view that given the diversity of cultural background and historical experiences of different political societies, their social and political development will follow different routes. Let us briefly examine some of their ideas.

De Tocqueville was deeply impressed by the manner in which the United States, a young country without many traditions or a long history, was able, with ease and minimum friction, to implement the principle of 'the sovereignty of the people'. Such a principle, along with the norms of equality, participation and achievement, exercised enormous influence on the United States' subsequent political development.[8] They also deeply influenced her laws, the behaviour of her people on both sides of the power divide, and above all, helped shape the nature of her political society. Such influences operated along with the vision and quality which her founding fathers brought to bear in building and operating her new political institutions.

As opposed to that, a number of European countries were 'devastated' by their efforts to restructure their political institutions on parallel lines. In this case, their historical past did not make the job any easier. In the case of France, in particular, her kings, aristocracy, men of learning, church, peasants and other groups – from the beginning of the twelfth century – failed to create the social and political conditions for an incremental change in liberal directions. Not even by means of the cataclysmic French Revolution of 1789, in some ways inspired by the American Revolution a decade earlier, could France make a total break with her past. While her revolution did destroy aristocratic and feudal institutions, it nevertheless allowed others to persist.[9]

So then the actual consequences of the two great revolutions, American and French, on which de Tocqueville wrote his two classics, produced diverse results. While in the former there was a departure from old conditions, there was also a return with a difference, in the case of the latter, to pre-revolutionary conditions. To de Tocqueville, the understanding of the actualities of political societies, as they develop historically, cannot be left to pure theorists. Such an understanding calls for a deeper grasp of social conditions. On his part, therefore, de Tocqueville went into great details about the actual implementation of laws in the post-revolutionary period, to point out the limited nature of real change in French local administration.[10]

Max Weber identified in much greater detail, probably more than any other social theorist, the range of conditioning forces in a country's economic and political development. For this purpose he concentrated first on religion, along with economic factors, and then on their interplay in shaping the attitudes of people towards the pursuit of their social and economic objectives.

To Weber, religions, particularly in those historical periods when they were of primary social importance, shaped 'man's attitude towards the world', and economic life within it.[11] Economic forces gave concrete expression to that attitude, and when firmed up, acted as the most powerful factor in determining the course of historical development of any society. Together with these forces, the various 'rationalities' which are implicit in legal and political institutions also played their part in shaping the peculiarities of the social and economic organisations of different societies.

To illustrate this argument, Max Weber made an ambitious attempt to identify what he called 'the economic ethic' of the major religions of the world such as Confucianism, Hinduism, Buddhism, Christianity, Islam and Judaism. According to him, there is implicit in these religions the 'economic ethic' which shaped 'the practical impulse for action' of the people who subscribed to it. Such an ethic influenced certain strata of followers of those religions and they, in turn, influenced the rest of society.[12]

In his seminal work on *The Protestant Ethic and the Spirit of Capitalism,* Max Weber pointed out how certain reinterpretations of economic activity and its rewards, undertaken by various Puritan denominations, affected and spurred the economic activity of the entrepreneurial class. These denominations, and, in particular, Calvinism, turned the pursuit of wealth from a mere 'advantage' to some kind of 'duty', with well-deserved rewards of its own. There was, in the words of R. H. Tawney, a 'change of moral standards' which 'canonized . . . economic virtues', making 'capitalism . . . the social counterpart of Calvinist theology'.[13]

Initially capitalism benefitted from, and even actively used, the Calvinist emphasis on the virtues of asceticism, hard work, thrift, etc. Later on it developed its own rationalities to ensure support for its own dynamism.[14]

In his subsequent work, *General Economic History,* Max Weber examined the growth of various social and political institutions in Western Europe which not only facilitated the phenomenal growth of capitalism but also helped to sustain it. Different kinds of land tenure, the sharing of the fruits of agricultural labour, industry, mining, crafts, guilds, shop production, increasingly unrestricted commerce, nded role of money and banking, etc., were identified by nim as historical forces which shaped the social and political institutions of different societies differently. With the help of such indicators, Max Weber was able to identify differences not only between Western and non-Western societies but also between Western societies.[15]

But over and above these, what had, in fact, made the necessary difference to the growth of various political economies of certain Western countries was an additional group of economic factors ranging from means of production, trading market, access to labour market, rational capital accounting, colonial expansion, etc. Together with them, the growth of the modern state, expert administrative officialdom, rational law, impersonal authority, cities and a changing concept of citizenship (from city-dweller to political participant) helped build the social and political organisation of the countries of Western Europe.[16]

Max Weber's writings, which had an enormous influence on all branches of the social sciences, failed to sensitise a generation of scholars researching and writing on political development. One reason for this was that unlike them he was continually and painstakingly engaged in enriching his theoretical formulations so as not to miss out on the identification of complex differences between societies. For him, the more we were able to identify differences between societies, the deeper became our appreciation of their actualities. Such an ethic of sensitivity to actualities became secondary at the hands of scholars who were in a hurry to claim the universal validity of their much less sophisticated, rarely pretested or subsequently refined theories.

Thorstein Veblen sensitised us to the problem of 'borrowing' technological developments and institutions from other countries.[17] He maintained that a country that borrows from another may miss out on the consequential social change which followed in the wake of whatever was evolved by the source country. For example, the social change which occurred in Britain as a result of the gradual industrialisation of her economy could not be 'borrowed' by a country which merely imitated Britain's technology. In fact, there is no such thing as a country being able to 'borrow' social change which occurs in another country, as a result of its gradual indigenous development. When one country 'borrows' from another what in fact it does is to graft the borrowed component on to whatever it already has. In the course of time such grafting will inevitably produce its own consequential social change. Such a change will nevertheless have its own peculiarities. Veblen used this argument to point out that Germany in the nineteenth century could only borrow British technology but not the liberal social and political change which occurred in Britain as a result of her own industrial revolution. For Veblen, a similar argument could be made about Japan. She too 'borrowed' technology from the Western countries, but the kind of social change which her external borrowing produced was vastly different from the countries from where it was 'borrowed'.

Joseph Schumpeter was concerned with yet another aspect of diversity, namely, the phenomenon of incompatibility between what was borrowed and what was indigenous, and the social consequences of such a mismatch. For him the norms and attitudes implicit in indigenous organisation do not easily change with the advent of what comes in from outside. And they seem to persist like 'coins that do not readily melt'.[18]

In the post Second World War period, and particularly since the emergence of a number of new countries, the incidence of borrowing by the developing countries from the developed has vastly expanded. Quite often what has been 'borrowed' has to coexist – in a semi-integrated or unintegrated way, and sometimes in situations of conflict – with what has been indigenously produced. Consequently, Bendix drew the attention of scholars studying development to what he called 'amalgams of tradition and modernity'.[19] That is what makes the process of development different in different societies.

The kind of concepts with which the phenomenon of development is to be studied, Bendix further argued, are deeply rooted in the experiences of a few Western countries. Since the 'industrialisation' and 'modernisation' of Western societies took place simultaneously with urbanisation, education, social mobility, the growth of responsible government, and, above all, *laissez-faire* capitalism, most of the conceptual terms treat this latter set of factors as a precondition of the former.[20] Moreover, such factors are also treated as preconditions of liberal political development. So great has been the assumed causal relationship between them that some kind of insensitivity to the world of actualities is generated, whereby social reality of a different kind is ignored simply because it is different from Western experience. Often, therefore, it is supposed not to exist.

To summarise, de Tocqueville, Weber, Veblen, Schumpeter and Bendix, with their variety of emphases on the need to recognise the diversity of political societies, rendered a valuable service to the students of political development. Unfortunately, this aspect of their contribution has not received sufficient attention. For one thing, they all want us to look beyond the neat and oversimplified unilinear theoretical explanations of development to the unfamiliar and baffling variety of non-Western social and political reality. That in turn requires a careful examination of our very conceptual tools of inquiry and of the corpus of theoretical knowledge in general. On such an examination depends the possibility of their refinement, reformulation and enhanced adequacy.

III THE POLITICAL ACTUALITY OF SOME OF THE NON-WESTERN COUNTRIES OF SOUTH ASIA, AFRICA, THE MIDDLE EAST AND LATIN AMERICA

Various political societies offer evidence of different kinds of influence in shaping their public institutions. Even when their legal and political institutions, bureaucracy, army, system of education, economic and financial structures, etc., are emulated or borrowed from a common source, they come to acquire different characteristics of their own in different countries. Despite the superficial resemblance of such institutions at the formal level, in their actual operations they are deeply influenced by the social and cultural conditions within which they function. Thus, for example, the four countries of South Asia, namely, India, Pakistan, Bangladesh and Sri Lanka – with long phases of common historical experience and similar cultural roots, with an identical exposure to British political ideals, public institutions and educational system, and also with a more or less similar choice of political institutions in their post-colonial period – have developed, in a span of four decades since independence, legal and political institutions which are different from each other's.

While the fact of their diversity is recognised at the level of commonsense, and specifically at the level of individual country studies, it is often assumed in generalised theories of political development that they would evolve towards a greater degree of similarity to each other, in their efforts to modernise themselves, than their differences at present warrant. In this section we shall argue that only by recognising the diversity between political societies would we be able to have a more realistic understanding of their political actualities. Only through a clearer understanding of their diversity and actuali y would we be able to evolve a notion of what I have called in Chapter 4 the 'public minimum' applicable to all political societies.

The political actualities of India, which we shall examine in much greater detail in the next chapter, have had their roots in her classical civilisation, the polytheistic and relativistic emphases of Hinduism, India's conquest by invaders and the consequent coexistence of several belief and cultural systems, the neglect of social organisation and its deeply institutionalised hierarchy, condemning a section of her society to incredible indignity and humiliation, social and religious reform movements to rebuild her society, a fascination for liberal political ideals as a corrective to her unequal social order, a movement for national independence spread over a century, the political mobilisation of her people on an unprecedented scale in history, the extraordinary quality of a large number of the political elite, a deep commitment to the ideals of democracy, secularism and social change, the involvement and political learning through democratic process, the explosion of education, a cynical opportunism to derive personal benefit from India's enormous potential for development, and so forth. These together have contributed, among other things, to India's enormous internal diversity and the awesome complexity of her social and political life. Amongst students of political development, India is often referred to as an example of ultimate complexity defying attempts at both generalisation and comparison. As a society she also reminds us that there are no shortcuts to the understanding of her political activities, least of all by means of inferences drawn from supposedly parallel experiences. More about this later.

Pakistan began her political career as a modern constitutional state with the hope of creating social conditions which would facilitate the pursuit of the ideals of Islam. In that respect, Pakistan, unlike other Muslim countries, has been a *rechtstaat*, a state with its own sovereign legal and political institutions. While in the bulk of Muslim countries of the Middle East any proposal for the creation of a modern constitutional state gets embroiled in fanatical religious denunciations and controversies among the clerics and lay scholars, the two founding fathers of Pakistan, namely Jinnah and Liaquatali Khan, laid the foundation of a composite constitutional state which could guarantee conditions for the pursuit of Islamic ideals.

In the creation of Pakistan, religion as the basis of the two nations, Hindu and Muslim, played an important part. While the Indians, who were determined to build a secular society for themselves, rejected that theory, and accepted the partition of India only as the price of their freedom from British rule, the Pakistanis made religion the starting point of their nationhood.

Depending on political circumstance, different views on the relationship between the state and religion surfaced in Pakistan at different times. Among others the following two were important: first, since the nation was created for the pursuit of the ideals of Islam, such ideals should be assimilated and guaranteed in the constitution; and, second, the need to build a strong Islamic state so that it could not only practise the ideals of Islam but also defend itself with the support of religion. Soldiers in Pakistan, in and out of office, often used the second argument to justify their capture and retention of power.

It is difficult to project as to when the problem of the relationship between the state and religion will be resolved in Pakistan. What cannot be ignored, however, is its importance in the political development of Pakistan. Apart from the controversy over whether Islam as a religion should remain only as a normative source for the general direction of a modern society or become the very basis of all its laws and institutions, the presence of such an unresolved controversy has prevented the growth of an effective political process which can compel her rulers to act in accordance with the rule of law, respond to public demands and render accountability for their performance in office.

The political actualities of Pakistan are thus shaped by a different mould from all other neighbouring countries. Historically, culturally, educationally, and in terms of political and economic aspirations, Pakistan and India, along with Bangladesh and Sri Lanka, have many things in common. In a genuine sense these countries constitute an international reference group. What happens in one of those countries is closely watched by the rest. Their individual success becomes a source of envy for the rest and failure provides a warning that it could happen to them. While the Indians envied the economic development of Pakistan during the early years of Ayyub Khan's authoritarian regime, the Pakistanis have envied the stability of Indian democracy and in particular India's ability to expel Indira Gandhi for her authoritarian policies in 1977.

Despite a common heritage and aspirations, and despite the presence of an international reference group inducing the countries of South Asia to keep a close watch on their neighbours, the political actualities of Pakistan have been shaped by those organisations and forces which could fill the vacuum left behind by the unresolved relationship between religion and state, on the one hand, and the uncrystallised institutions of government and politics, on the other. The main beneficiaries of such a vacuum are the bureaucracy, the army, large landholders, a select number of families with commercial and industrial undertakings, and clerics. Together, they have successfully subverted several attempts to develop an effective political process whereby public decisions could be made by elected officials rather than by the nominees of these powerful forces. Neither the intellectuals, nor the professional classes, nor indeed the political elites representing a large number of regional and national parties have been able effectively to mobilise the people of Pakistan, in order to give them a fresh opportunity to rebuild the institutions of government and politics so as to have the rule of law administered by elected public officials. Apart from the ruthlessness of military rulers, the failure of political elites to come together in a spirit of give and take for a common purpose has been largely responsible for the continuation of illiberal regimes in Pakistan.

Bangladesh, like Pakistan, is another predominantly Muslim country in South Asia. And like the latter, it too went through a tortuous cycle of military and civilian rule in a short span of time. But unlike Pakistan and the bulk of Muslim countries, Bangladesh has been less troubled by the Islamic compulsions of having to reflect the main tenets of *Quoran* and *Sharia* in her systems of law, government, economy, education, etc. While such a compulsion does exist at the level of pious believers – that one is not a good Muslim unless one lives strictly according to religious teaching – the pressure for moving in that direction is confined to staunch believers, mullahs and a few politicians.

The subnationalism of the Bengalis, which was at the root of the creation of Bangladesh, was expressed through a secular idiom of culture and the fair distribution of resources between the east and west wings of what was formerly Pakistan. It was also emphasised through a liberal democratic idiom of the people's right to participate in decisions which affected their lives. In the series of crises which this young nation went through – the war of independence, coups and military takeovers – her leaders as well as her people did not abandon a secular approach to their problem.

At the same time, however, her political elite and intellectuals failed to tone down their excessive criticism, obstructionism and mutual distrust. The British colonial administration, the exploitative administration of West Pakistan, the controversial policies of Mujib, the father of the nation, the presence of a big and easily dislikable neighbour such as India, the weight of enormous population in a country with limited resources, the vagaries of the weather, etc., became objects of perennial criticism and griping. Bangladesh's leading men in public life, therefore, took far too long to realise that, as a free people, in the final analysis, *they* will be required to solve their own problems rather than forever go in search of someone else to blame for their share of misfortunes.

The political development of Bangladesh, together with the solution of her colossal economic problems, depend on the ability of her political elite and intellectuals to tone down their fierce individualism, and learn, through a spirit of give and take, the difficult lesson of working together. Even when that is achieved, the gigantic problem of keeping the army out of civilian affairs will require an enormous effort on the part of everyone concerned, especially the uncompromising politicians.

The problems of the political development of Bangladesh, then, are the problems of a paucity of resources, fierce individualism, squabbling politicians, ambitious soldiers, and a failure to strike a balance between what is normatively desirable and what is politically possible. In that sense it is materially different from her close neighbours with whom she has shared so much of her history, culture, exposure to Western influence and legal and political institutions.

Within the subcontinent there is also Sri Lanka, with a remarkable record of the survival of liberal political institutions. Sri Lanka has a very high rate of literacy, universal adult suffrage going back to the pre-independence period, several general elections and peaceful changes of government, and a voting turnout of more than 80 per cent. Barring exceptions, she has also refrained from engaging in the zero-sum game, whereby electorally victorious politicians inflict a great many disadvantages and hardships on the vanquished, which is so very noticeable in developing countries.

In the 1950s, Sri Lanka embarked on a phase of re-Buddhification of her population after centuries of Christian rule. Later on, her politicians also wanted to make Buddhism the state religion. Fortunately, that was not pressed too far. Nevertheless, she did face a reaction from her minorities, in particular, the Tamil Hindus who constitute a sizeable and active minority. Over the years, and particularly during British rule, the dynamic and hardworking Tamils built positions of economic advantage and employment for themselves. The post-independence public policies gradually chipped away at those advantages, enhancing their feelings of insecurity and inequality. The radicals among the Tamils saw no other way but a separate state for themselves. This resulted in a series of problems relating to Tamil citizenship, economic investment in the region, employment, violent clashes and the internationalisation of the problem. The treatment of the Tamil minority deeply tarnished the image of Sri Lanka as an humane and genuinely accommodating liberal political society.

Despite the crises of the 1980s, and of earlier periods, Sri Lanka remains one of the most successful democracies of the non-Western world. And the quality of her public life, together with her political development, is vitally influenced by her cultural legacies, the norms of Buddhist philosophy, her ethnic composition, a commitment to liberal political values, and, above all, her political leadership.

The four South Asian countries, namely, India, Pakistan, Bangladesh and Sri Lanka, despite a number of common features in their history, culture, exposure to British colonial experience and Western education, thus began to manifest, shortly after attaining independence, different problems relating to their own specific course of political development.

The two liberal democracies among them, namely India and Sri Lanka, began to reveal their own differences. India, because of her awesome cultural, social and religious diversity, began to put an enormous premium on secularism, mutual respect and adjustment, and on political skills which are addressed to coexistence and composite support for public office and policy. The conditions imposed by such a diversity, together with India's firmly institutionalised and intractable social hierarchy, created a genuine respect and longing for Western liberal political ideals among India's own political elite. These then sat very well with the implications for broad humanistic equality, at a normative level, in Hinduism as a belief system. It nevertheless ran counter to the hierarchical social organisation implicit in Hindu society. The political elites of such a society secretly hoped that through the equalitarian force of a foreign liberal ideology they would be able to get over the embarrassing social inequality. The complex diversity of India, the peculiarities of the belief system and social organisation, and above all the deep appreciation of liberal values by her political elite, have together influenced and shaped the operations of her public institutions, the drift of political development and the quality of public life in general.

Sri Lanka, on the other hand, being far less diverse in her internal composition, made Buddhist humanistic ideals the source of her social and political guidance, instead of Western liberalism. This provoked its own reaction amongst her minorities. In her political development, therefore, the ideals of religion, as a good enough source of her liberal development, effectively competed against foreign ideology. Such a shift did not make her more liberal than she had been. On the contrary, it created problems of coexistence and tolerance of people subscribing to different belief systems. The shift to a widely-subscribed belief system of Buddhism, its use and abuse by politicians, and the repercussions of all this on Sri Lanka's problems of coexistence with religious minorities, have together deeply influenced the quality of her public life and political development in general.

The Muslim countries of South Asia, namely Pakistan and Bangladesh, recently separated from each other, present their own political diversity. They differ not only from the other two countries of the region but also from each other. The political development of both of them has been seriously interrupted by ambitious soldiers who themselves later on turned politicians and sought popular political support. The justification provided for military intervention in each case was different. In Pakistan such a justification ranged from the need to build an infant state; to protect it against a covetous neighbour, India; to protect it against squabbling and corrupt politicians; and, above all, to facilitate the implementation of the tenets of Islam. In Bangladesh, however, religion was played down by the soldiers. The military intervention there was couched in terms of the need to remove corrupt politicians and eventually establish a more viable democracy. In both cases, due to repeated military takeovers, the experiments in liberal democracy, whereby people learn over a period of time the valuable political lessons of how to guard their individual, group and community interests by making use of the self-governing and self-educating political process, were not allowed to get off the ground.

The countries of South Asia, then, despite their geographical contiguity, shared historical past and cultural traits, exposure to common influences from the West, etc., gave rise to processes of political development which were so very different from one another's. Unless we zero in on the actualities of such processes, any general theory of political development is not going to tell us much about them.

The countries of Africa – with wide variations in their historical background, ethnic composition, economic resources, extent of political mobilisation during the pre- and post-colonial period, and, above all, the quality of political leadership – present a highly diverse picture of actual and potential political development.

The bulk of African countries, with a few exceptions, have had effective movements for national independence for less than a quarter of a century. Most of them, therefore, had a limited mobilisation of their own people. Moreover, such a mobilisation was confined, by and large, as in most developing countries, to a few urban centres. In rural areas, it did not go beyond the leading men and tribal chiefs, if any. In most such countries, therefore, the agitational aspects of national movement – which imparted a vital political education in civil rights, political participation, the seeking of response and accountability from those in public office, all of inestimable value in the post-independence period – touched only limited segments of society. The rest were either marginally involved or remained as spectators joining in cultural and ceremonial activities.

Political education through political agitation and mobilisation was thus confined to a very limited political elite drawn from the ranks of tribal chiefs, retired bureaucrats, journalists, lawyers, doctors and expatriates. After independence most of these were directly involved in managing various public institutions. Consequently, very few of the first-generation political elite stayed outside public office to oversee the performance of their countrymen in office. Those that did remain outside public office and/or were thrown out of power, were either rendered silent by means of threats and incarceration or were forced to flee the country.

Political leaders of the post-independence period, who had denounced in no uncertain terms the unresponsiveness and ruthlessness of the colonial administration, often reestablished the political distance between themselves and the people they governed, and also brought back several repressive measures with greater ferocity than before. Public office was treated, by most of these leaders, neither as electorally mandated, to be used strictly in accordance with law, nor as a matter of trust and responsibility, nor indeed as an occasion to set an example, and build tradition, to govern the future ruler–ruled relationships. Such an approach to public authority did not allow the cultivation of respect for law, orderly criticism and peaceful change of government. In a large number of African countries, dissidents and critics learned to remain silent to save their own lives or joined plotters to overthrow governments. In all of this what did not develop, and in fact suffered a reversal in the period following agitation against colonial rule, was the respect for public institutions, on both sides of the power divide, the independence of bureaucracy and judiciary, a free press, and party organisations which would share the dos and don'ts of liberal democracy.

Few countries of Africa have successfully cultivated a positive attitude towards political parties in or out of office. If and when elections were held, competition for power assumed the character of an ethnic or tribal conflict. For the competing parties in each electoral conflict, therefore, much more than public office was at stake. Those who won in elections wanted to make provisions against future loss. And those who lost did not want to acknowledge the legitimacy of the electorally victorious. Consequently, in a number of countries of Africa the aftermath of elections was often a sordid affair, with all the characteristics of a ruthless zero-sum game.

Furthermore, in the bulk of African countries there had been the difficulty of building public institutions, of either government or politics, on crosscutting ethnic, religious or regional lines.

Given such experiences, the political development of African countries needs to be studied not only with reference to their diversity and the actuality of particular problems but also in terms of what can be done to minimise the deleterious influence exercised by some of the social and cultural problems.

Different countries of Africa – whether black or multiracial, anglophone or francophone – given their internal composition, colonial legacy and exposure to a metropolitan system of education and political ideals, have come up with different directions of actual or potential political development. Even two countries such as Kenya and Nigeria, with an exposure to a common system of laws, political ideals, education, etc., during the colonial period, have come up with directions of political development which are dissimilar.

Kenya, at the end of her colonial rule, made a superhuman effort to lay the foundation of a multiracial society within a constitutional framework. Her three racial groups, namely the overwhelming number of Africans, the English with their organisational and industrial skills, and the Indians with their commercial acumen, together laid the foundation of independent Kenya. Her highly accommodationist policy, and the spirit of give and take in forging new relationships and new bonds of coexistence, have had their own indigenous critics. Periodically, under pressure from her own extremists, who believe that Kenya had to pay too high a price for her independence, there are many doubts expressed as to the wisdom of her decision to give so many concessions to non-Africans. Such doubts and criticisms also generate pressure for the Africanisation of her economy, bureaucracy and institutions. While it has been relatively easy to Africanise Kenya's bureaucracy, the extension of the same process to the other two areas has not been resorted to for fear of economic setbacks and political instability. Consequently, her accommodationist policies, with all their hopes and fears, with periodic mounting of racial tensions, remain precarious.

In the political field, Kenya, despite her commitment to liberal political values, took the retrograde step of making herself a one-party state. While such a move provided a preeminent position to certain tribal groups over others, it nevertheless deprived Kenya of the continued opportunity of establishing political institutions which cut across ethnic and racial ties and increasingly building a unique political society in Africa with a higher measure of tolerance, sense of security and mutually enriching diversity.

Nigeria too paid heavily for her inability to build political institutions which cut across the ethnic, religious and regional divides. During their freedom struggle, the Nigerians were able to build a broad-based national movement. Once the overall aim of independence was achieved, the political elite of Nigeria, instead of building new public institutions across various divisions, started cultivating, and exploiting, various divisive loyalties. Under the circumstances, Nigeria's elections were viewed by the average man, not as a rhetorical and theatred competition for power, or a special kind of conflict, but as a clash between rival ethnic and regional groups going back to their past. Thus each election, instead of strengthening the roots of coexistence, did considerable harm to them.

After the tragic and fratricidal Biafran cessionist civil war, and a number of humiliating military interventions, Nigeria made a determined effort to rebuild her institutions of government and politics on multiethnic and multiregional lines during the election of 1983. But by that time, the poor performance of Nigeria's economy, the decline in revenues from oil, the spread of corruption, etc., gave fresh justification to her army to intervene.

Thus Kenya, the only surviving liberal state of Africa, and Nigeria, repeatedly trying to learn the political lesson to bolster up her fragile but potentially liberal institutions after every military coup, realised that not only do they need a highly accommodationist approach to evolving public policies, to be able to obtain a cross-section of support for their policies, but that economically too they will have to do better than in the past. Their improved economic performance, *as* liberal states, will give an increased stake to their thinking men and women in their continued survival.

Once again, then, the political actualities of the countries of Africa require an appreciation of their own unique problems which any generalised theory of political development is likely to ignore.

The countries of the Middle East, unlike those of Asia and Africa, are far more influenced by their belief system and cultural forces. The reasons for such an influence are as follows. In Islam, unlike in most other major belief systems, the details of various other related systems, or in this case subsystems, i.e. economic, legal, political and social, are specifically indicated. Islam as a religion thus contains a body of principles and practical directions which affect not only the religious activity of its believers but also their system of laws, form of government, economic structure and social organisation in general. These principles and directions provide an holistic system subsuming within it other subsystems. Moreover, the compliance of any particular subsystem with the specific direction laid down by the belief system is eagerly, passionately and sometimes fanatically sought. By definition, therefore, one is not a good enough Muslim unless one also allows the message of Islam to permeate all walks of individual and social life.[21]

Few developing countries, after attaining their independence, specifically or explicitly sought to put their religious house in order for fear of resentment. What most of them have done, by inadvertence or design, however, is gradually to delir k all other related systems and bring them within the purview of the wider politico-legal secular system. Changes were then introduced in those related systems as a matter of concern to everyone. That in turn helped generate in some political societies a questioning attitude towards the excessive claims of religion.

In Muslim countries, barring a few exceptions, however, such an approach has provoked different degrees of resistance from believers, clerics and scholars. Together they have succeeded in discouraging long overdue changes in the field of the rights of women, education, laws, the economy and public life in general.

One of the greatest casualties, in that respect, has been what can be vaguely referred to as an arena where effective political process, addressed to public concerns, is generated. Such an arena has not been allowed to demarcate itself wherein an individual can express his legitimate political concerns about those in public office, and seek their performance, response and accountability by means of effective, and what are commonly considered to be legitimate, forms of political action.

The main beneficiaries of the non-emergence of such an arena were the people in political authority. The lay and clerical segments of Middle Eastern societies often made pious pronouncements, rather than become involved themselves effectively in the political process as an effective countervailing force against the excesses of political rulers.[22]

In the absence of effective constraints, religious, constitutional and/or political, those who get into power – by means of hereditary succession, tribal arrangement, election or military takeover – often succeed in building for themselves enormous networks of personalised power in which family, lineage, marriage and above all, who one knows, count the most.[23]

What is more, the countries which tried to minimise the influence of religion in society such as Turkey, Egypt and Tunisia, paid heavily in terms of their influence and friendship with neighbouring Muslim states. Attempts to introduce some measure of secularism were seen not as a way of making the pursuit of one's faith a private matter between the individual and his god, but as opening doors to other religious ideas. Under the circumstances secularism, which to some extent depends on the Judeo-Christian component of liberalism, was often pointed out by Islamic scholars as accepting the principles of rival religions. Such an acceptance, they argued, would give additional advantages to other religions over their own.

The actualities of political development of the countries of the Middle East thus hinge on the two basic issues: the nuances of the enmeshing of religion and politics; and the equally complex reality of attempts, and impediments to them, at creating a legitimate area of politics where effective political pressure can be generated and brought to bear within a constitutional and commonly accepted framework, in order to seek responses and accountability from those in public office.

At the two ends of the mix of religion and politics we have the example of Saudi Arabia, which tries to embody and pursue the puristic traditions of Islam, as formulated by Wahhabism; and Turkey, which tries to use the strong arm of the state, inherited through the centralist and activist state of the Ottoman empire, to modernise her society.

The Wahhabistic Islam has blended itself effectively with the norms and consultative mechanisms of Saudi Arabia's strongest tribal group, namely the Bedouins. The clerical order of Wahhabism acts as a consultative body and an informal judicial organisation to review the Islamic soundness of *all* legislations, practices and institutions. Consequently, neither the tribal consultative organisation nor the Wahhabist clerical–judicial body have so far felt the need to reorder the existing political arrangements of Saudi society.

In the past few years, however, there has been an enormous growth of education, oil industry, bureaucracy and new institutions. These together have also given rise to a new managerial and technocratic elite, a large segment of which was trained abroad. The individuals within such a group have begun to play an important part in various consultative processes. Nevertheless, given the deep-rooted traditions of Saudi Arabia, this elite will have to work within the established institutions and mechanisms before it can bring about any appreciable change in them from within. Meanwhile, what Saudi Arabia will not tolerate, and demonstrably has not tolerated in recent years, is the transplanting of new legal and political institutions from elsewhere. Consequently, for the foreseeable future whatever administrative and political development that takes place will be cast within the matrices of what already exists.[24]

At the other end of the spectrum there is Turkey, the only Middle Eastern country to make a conscious attempt to break away from the past only to find herself uncomfortably placed between the conflicting demands of traditional culture and modern ways of doing things. Unlike other countries of the region, Turkey inherited a well-established state uninhibited by religious considerations. Consequently, it was natural for her to make use of the legal and political machinery of the state to modernise herself.

Certain segments of the Turkish intelligentsia and army, which were deeply attracted to Western social and political ideals and institutions, wanted to bring about changes on similar lines in their own society. When their activity gained ground in the mid nineteenth century, they were dubbed 'the Young Turks'. They became effective when Mustafa Kemal took charge of the country. Together, they introduced a series of far-reaching changes in the educational, religious and political life of society.

One of the goals of 'the Young Turks' was to establish liberal political institutions in Turkey. Unfortunately, they depended far too much on measures to be introduced from the top, without effectively mobilising the people to be able to appreciate the nature and significance of various reforms.

More than half a century has passed since those reforms were introduced and new political institutions established, but the people of Turkey have yet to learn, assimilate and practise the underlying dos and don'ts of those institutions. Despite various elections, political crises, military takeovers and fresh attempts to restore democratic practices, usually in that order, Turkey has not been able to teach her people the much-needed political skills of accommodation and compromise, in operating liberal political institutions. While liberal institutions facilitate the expression and pursuit of diverse goals, they cannot function if every time such a diversity results in uncompromising polarity or plurality. Of necessity, therefore, liberal institutions depend on the initial expression of differences and then a search for accommodationist solutions of at least some of those differences.

Differences expressed during elections in Turkey often create unbridgeable gulfs between the people and their party organisations. Turkey's people often fail to view the rhetorical, theatred and party-engineered conflicts as special kinds of conflicts for the purpose of elections only. Electoral conflicts acquire in Turkey a deep and unhealthy social significance. They therefore often prevent the resumption of normal social life in the post-election periods. Contending sides continue to brand each other as *düshman* (enemy).[25]

Whenever contending political groups and organisations make political institutions unworkable, the army moves in, dissolves those groups and organisations, debars certain political leaders from active politics, introduces some reforms, and tries to give another lease of life to democracy. Turkey, therefore, has created a curious situation of having to depend on the army, each time, to dissolve the groups of uncompromising contenders, and give democracy yet another try.

The political development of Turkey has thus been contingent upon the ability of her people to learn the dos and don'ts of operating liberal political institutions. That alone will break the tortuous cycle of civilian and military rule. In learning such dos and don'ts several countries have drawn a large number of lessons from their experiences, conventional morality, religion, culture and, above all, pragmatic commonsense.[26] The extraordinary delay on the part of Turkey to draw such lessons from her own cultural and practical experiences makes her case unique. Scholars have yet to throw light on that phenomenon.

Let us now take into account some of the general characteristics of Latin American political societies which, as scholars argue, have been neglected by general theories of political development. Since they are unique to the countries of Latin America, those political development theories, which are grounded only in the experiences of Western countries, tend to ignore them.

The countries of Latin America, because of their chronic political instability, illiberal regimes, coups, superpower intrigues, interference by multinationals, etc., have become objects of derision, indifference or at best a patchy understanding. Such a situation was not lost on Latin American scholars, indigenous as well as expatriate, and in recent years, through their scholarly writings they have succeeded in pointing out the biases and distortions in the understanding of political actualities of that region. Some of the major points made by such scholars, taking into account the historical experiences and cultural conditions of that region, are as follows: historically speaking, a large number of Latin American countries have been heirs to an Iberic-Latin tradition which emphasises a closer relationship between the state and society. Such an emphasis makes the region vastly different from the countries of Western Europe and North America.

Moreover, culturally those countries have been influenced by the religio-political liberalism of St Thomas rather than the liberalism of the West which was an offshoot of *laissez-faire* capitalism and individualism. The individual, emphasised in Thomistic philosophy, is an integral part of his community rather than pitted against it as in the West. Consequently, in the absence of traditions of individual rights – the individual as the basis of polity, the individual versus the state, all of these in the Western style – the countries of Latin America have developed large collectivities or corporations such as union, party, church, army and bureaucracy, which have entered into the political arena and competed for their share of political power. And so far as the average individual is concerned, he seeks his self-realisation, security and the protection of his interests within these large corporations and their interplay in society, economy and polity.

Only recently have Latin American politicians and scholars started taking an interest in Western liberalism and Marxism; how that will affect and reshape their Iberic-Latin traditions still remains to be seen.

In a sense, the tradition of governance in the countries of Latin America was shaped by the fact of their own insulation from the various powerful currents of social and political ideas, and of institutional changes, that had fundamentally altered political relationships in the countries of the West. These currents, of far-reaching importance, were represented by the Reformation, the growth of constitutionalism at the end of the social contract debate, and the political ideals, of lasting value, dramatically projected by the French Revolution. The insulation of countries of Latin America from these and other powerful currents of ideas and experiences were characterised by a Latin American scholar as *the four absences:* the absence of feudal contractualism; of religious nonconformity; of early industrial revolution and its social consequences; and the absence of the impact of the political ideals of the French Revolution.[27] These, together, significantly altered the social and political organisation of the countries of Western Europe and, under their influence, those of many others. In the absence of such an influence, the countries of Latin America followed their own course, and developed a strong 'centralist' character whereby the state came to acquire a predominant role in society, economy, culture, education and in other compartments of political life.

Latin American scholars, who were dissatisfied with the superficial manner in which the complex phenomenon of 'corporatism' was treated in the literature on political development, have themselves come out with a rich analysis of the nuances, operational peculiarities and their significance for various political societies in that region. According to them, the countries of Latin America are a *terra incognita* for political analysts, and especially for those who depend entirely on the corpus of theoretical knowledge developed in the West. For a good understanding of the phenomenon of 'corporatism', these scholars argue, one ought to examine the actualities of the operations of various 'corporations' rather than seek to understand them by means of extraneous theories.[28]

One of the most puzzling aspects of Latin American politics is the frequency of coups in that region. A coup, by definition, at least in Western political science literature, is regarded as a symptom of a political malaise in the body politic; to overcome it, its constituents are driven to resort to such a desperate remedy.

As opposed to that, some Latin American scholars argue that there is another way of looking at coups. Given the nature of their politics, where gradual political change becomes difficult, if not impossible, the countries of Latin America resort to coups as a means of realigning themselves politically, and thereby making their political order reflect more accurately the changes in society. That increasingly coups are becoming less and less violent, and most of them aim at bringing about changes in the top management and its policies.

Quite often the bulk of the population in such coups is neither affected
nor involved. Consequently, the question which these scholars raise
is whether coups can be equated with elections, given the political
actualities of Latin American countries. Moreover, sometimes coups
radically alter the drift of social and political direction in certain
countries. In that sense they become 'critical coups', similar to 'critical elections', which lay down a new direction for the political society to follow for a number of years.[29]

What is nevertheless true of the countries of Latin America is that
their institutions, and the unwritten and unstated dos and don'ts of
operating them, rarely get a chance to firm up in the face of coups
and their unpredictable frequency. Which in turn makes their politics a matter of effective mobilisation of people by 'corporations'. The
citizens, under the circumstances, are treated as recipients of what
comes along, after a balance between various 'corporations' has been
struck, rather than as participants and demanders of satisfaction of
their wants. Surely there are aspects of citizens which are not sub-
merged in 'corporations', and which can be adequately served by a
demand–response political process in which they have a role to play
as citizens.

What has been at the centre of Latin American politics is the state,
its manifold operations, interventions, importance and all-
pervasiveness. The actualities of such a state *presence* are missed out
by the social sciences, which are deeply rooted in Western political
experience, where the state's operations are far more limited. The
Anglo-Saxon countries, in particular, are far more concerned and
observant of society rather than the state. Consequently, the corpus
of theoretical knowledge, with the help of which we study political
development, often fails to register the complex role of the state in
the political societies of Latin American countries.[30]

Scholars of Latin American political studies thus remind us that
in the study of political development we have to go beyond liberal
political ideals to the actualities of political processes of various
countries and see what other kinds of needs of citizens they serve.
Maybe they satisfy an aspect of such wants which has been beyond
the experience of Western societies. Without minimising the importance of liberal ideals such as equality and participation, we should
also be able to identify and explain them. The first step in the direction of such an exploration, therefore, is to have a clearer view of
the actualities of their political processes and then understand them
not as a parallel of Western experience but as something different.

It is by understanding their actuality that we will be able to understand the unique purpose which they serve.

As the preceding pages suggest, the historical and cultural diversity of different societies was more readily acknowledged by scholars than was the possibility of their diverse political development. This was due to an assumption on their part that what contributed to societies being different from one another belonged to the pre-modern component within them. But once the process of modernisation caught hold of such societies, the finished product, at the other end of the process, would begin to resemble what exists in the West. In that connection we examined the ideas of scholars who argued, to the contrary, that the 'borrowing' and modernisation process, even among Western countries, did not produce identical political results. We have to guard against what Max Weber indicated as 'the fallacy of emanationism'. Such a note of caution also led us to the examination of the views of Bendix that we need to refine our own tools of conceptual analysis, which are deeply grounded in the political experience of a handful of Western countries. Such tools remain insensitive to the post-borrowing peculiarities of non-Western political societies.

The various political societies, despite borrowing their political ideals, institutions and practices from a common source, came out with diverse courses of their own possible political development. This was true even of those countries of South Asia which had so much in common with one another in their history, tradition and culture. What contributed to their essential differences calls for a closer examination of their post-colonial political development. Similarly, the differences between the countries of the Middle East, Africa, Latin America, where despite more or less similar problems of religion, ethnicity and Iberic-Latin heritage, respectively, different countries have registered a propensity towards a different course of actual or potential political development.

Such a realisation reinforces the need to examine the actualities of political development of various societies, along with their complexities and nuances, rather than ignore them, in order to validate previously arrived at grand theories of political development. Such a realisation may, no doubt, push back the process of formulating comprehensive theories of political development by years. But then within such a realisation also lies the possibility of following a course which will lead to a more reliable approach to the understanding of political development of non-Western societies.

3 Multilayered Political Societies and Conceptual Inadequacy

The terms, concepts and theories which are used in the social sciences to explain the social and political reality of the non-Western world are now being increasingly questioned as to their appropriateness and adequacy. This is because there is a growing volume of doubt – particularly among those political scientists and anthropologists who prefer to observe social reality by means of their field research, rather than get it theoretically prepackaged – concerning the sensitivity and effectiveness of the existing corpus of theoretical knowledge, which has been deeply rooted in Western cultural and historical experience. Such a body of knowledge lacks an assimilative disposition or effort required to understand the non-Western world, first of all, in its own contexts, and then in the contexts of concerns which are truly universal. What is often attempted, by way of analysis and explanation of the non-Western world, is what can be easily abstracted from its cultural contexts and fitted into previously developed, and almost always untested, theoretical formulations. In such an intellectual exercise what receives attention are the highly abstracted common denominators, devoid of their cultural contexts and significance, so that they may become reference points for a uniform theoretical explanation.

In his various writings Reinhard Bendix has repeatedly pointed out that the social sciences, which developed in England and which have since assimilated the social experiences of a few more Western countries, had difficulty in explaining, effectively, some of 'the late developers' among the industrialised countries of the West, namely Germany and Japan. Such a difficulty is further compounded when we take into account some of the 'new' countries of the non-Western world, which have tried to build an 'amalgam' of their traditional social institutions and what they borrowed from the West.[1]

Such a dissatisfaction with the existing corpus of theoretical knowledge has yet to develop into a fully-fledged controversy, despite the fact that there is a long tradition, since the days of classical Greece, of intellectual development through the idiom of controversy. Occasionally critiques of such theoretical knowledge appear in various journals, but they remain almost always unanswered, creating and prolonging the situation of precontroversy.

In this chapter we shall identify some of the complexities of the three major multilayered political societies such as the Indian, Chinese and Japanese and point out the conceptual inadequacy of the existing corpus of theoretical knowledge in understanding them. Efforts to understand their complexities are either distorted or watered down because of the built-in disposition in various theoretical approaches to touch upon only those aspects of non-Western societies which validate their own assertions and preconceptions.

India, China and Japan have multilayered[2] societies with several layers of culture, history and tradition in them. Such deposits have either fused, remained parallel, or have given rise to situations of conflict in those societies. Whatever may have been the case in different groups, situations or regions, these layers influence and shape the conduct of people in individual and public life, and the operations of social and political institutions. Sometimes the normative values implicit in some of those layers influence certain individuals and not others. Apart from that, the notions of right and wrong, social and political obligation, individual and group interest, etc., are all affected and shaped not only by indigenous experience, but also by what has been consciously borrowed from outside in recent years, and therefore has yet to settle down into yet another layer of experience. The unmanageability of such a dimension of complexity, together with our ignorance and naïveté, often persuade us to get on with our political analysis without taking them into account.

In this chapter we shall try to understand, very briefly, the influence exerted by the cultural deposits of these multilayered political societies on their political development in general. We shall also take into consideration specific instances of the inadequacy of certain conceptual tools in understanding specific aspects of their political development. The chapter is divided into the following parts: (i) India: multilayered political society; through the crucible of democratic process; and conceptual inadequacy; (ii) China: multilayered political society; political process; and conceptual inadequacy; (iii) Japan: group cohesion; and imposed democratic institutions. We shall now examine each of these subsections in some detail.

I   INDIA

Multilayered Political Society

The existing corpus of theoretical knowledge often tends to notice remarkable continuities in the growth of political ideals and public institutions, and a commensurate political behaviour to pursue those ideals and sustain those institutions, in the countries of the West. But corresponding cultural continuities, albeit frequently interrupted and breached, and their resumptions, with or without exogenous elements, are neither identified in the developing countries by the same theoretical corpus, nor are their influences recognised on the possible political development of those countries. On the contrary those theories often assume that developing countries, under the pressure of modernisation (i.e. Westernisation in this context) will either have registered a break from their past, or will do so in the future. Consequently, it is appropriate, and intellectually adequate from the point of view of such theories, to extend their own validity from the Western to the non-Western world. While scholars in the subdiscipline of political development have yet to address themselves seriously to the problems of such cultural continuities, with interruptions and resumptions, nevertheless their persistence and influence on the society and politics of new nations, despite various exogenous borrowings, cannot be denied.

Morris-Jones, a perceptive scholar of Indian politics, once remarked that India is a country where 'centuries coexist'. This had a reference to a different degree of advancement and development in different compartments of India's life. What still remains to be identified, and acknowledged, is that such a coexistence is horizontally and vertically spread. Individuals, groups and the political society of India as a whole continue to be influenced by normative emphases, notions of right and wrong, conceptions of freedom and obligations, and views on the ephemerality and illusion of human life – as given by philosophers and men of learning, experience and sacrifice – in her long and chequered history. Her classical civilisation, the period of prolonged glory, the Muslim period, the British period, the religious and social reform movements, the movement for national independence, the post-independence democratic experiments, and explorations into forms of political dissent and opposition, together constitute the many layers of culture and social and political strivings, and they continue to influence the disposition of her people to politics and their orientation to general.

While it is impossible causally to relate these tural determinants to specific kinds of political acti tions, an attempt will be made, in the following pa to identify the deep imprint left behind by some values and experiences on the political society of India as a whole.

The Indian civilisation, unlike most others, has been able to maintain a remarkable continuity and influence on her people despite wars, conquests and prolonged periods of social destabilisation. Her rich philosophical heritage, belief systems and traditional values encountered criticisms and challenges both from indigenous and exogenous sources, and survived by assimilating some of them despite manifold inconsistencies. And it patiently waited for the natural atrophy of those which it could not assimilate.

Since India's classical civilisation[3] dealt with the problems of the human mind and spirit, rather than with things material, neither the sheer passage of time nor the intrusion of other historical events could diminish the interest of her people in it. Consequently, even the oldest layer in India's political society continues to be meaningful to her people because of the kinds of problems to which it addressed itself.

The classical civilisation of India made its many-sided contribution particularly in the fields of art, literature, science and, above all, in philosophy. It gave rise to six highly developed schools of philosophy and took considerable pride in cultivating subtleties of intellectual effort and canons of reasoning. For such a civilisation, intellectual effort did not stop at identifying intellectual puzzles and their solutions but in extending a highly developed intellectual capacity to pursue mysteries of the human spirit and laws governing them. Such a capacity was also expected to understand the significance of human life and opportunity for *tirtha-kara* (bridge-building) between one phase of life and another. One of the major concerns of philosophy, therefore, was not merely the pursuit of pure intellectual problems but also the understanding of how to avoid the ills and illusions of life which distract us from its main purpose.[4]

Despite the passage of time and exposure to rival philosophical ideas through modern education, the intellectual pursuit of understanding the mysteries of the human spirit is still considered to be a worthwhile activity by the educated men and women of India.[5]

Such a background encourages the use of an idiom of expression

...hich is highly normative, and often didactic and unrelated to the realities of individual social and political limitations. Such a background, however, is not helpful in developing socially and politically realisable ideals by means of group effort. Such ideals, of pursuing matters of the spirit, with the help of a highly trained intellect, and the sacrifice of physical comforts, essentially become prescriptions for extraordinary individuals. While everyone talks about them in society, only a few can actually pursue them.

So far as the average individual in India is concerned, he admires the efforts of extraordinary men but then goes on to lead his own life in accordance with group standards and directions laid down by the religious texts, holymen and traditional leaders.

The unintended, but actual, classification of people in these two categories has persisted throughout Indian history, whereby extraordinary individuals attain great heights of achievement whereas the average do not advance very much.[6]

Then there are the six schools of Indian philosophy which competed and vied with one another for their own general acceptance. Nevertheless, what was common to all of them, as pointed out by India's leading philosopher, Radhakrishnan, is the view that 'vast periods of creation, maintenance and dissolution follow each other in endless succession'.[7]

Such a notion of reality directly affects any sense of permanence. Against such a background, material objects become impermanent, insubstantial and illusory; spiritual goals and objects appear timeless, real and worth pursuing. What appears to be there, and what is not easily perceived, has to be patiently pursued, understood and assimilated into our own being. The latter, therefore, requires a constant search on the part of the human mind and spirit in order to be able, increasingly, to know and understand. Simultaneously, it also requires an increasing detachment from the network of social relationships which are only worldly (illusory) ties, which create distortions and impose constraints on the pursuit of one's ultimate goal.

Later, we shall see that the Indian social and religious reform leaders of the nineteenth and twentieth centuries criticised the traditional attitude of not taking social reality seriously. A similar position was subsequently adopted by Mahatma Gandhi, against not taking the political reality seriously. He had maintained that political subjection and degradation could not allow any effective pursuit of the higher purposes of life, that social and political problems had to be tackled, and could be tackled, without giving up one's commitment to normative principles.

The classical civilisation of India put an enormous emphasis on the discovery and reformulation of moral and political relationships between the rulers and the ruled by means of an examination of ideals, precepts and ethical exhortations contained in epics and philosophical texts. This resulted in the development of state laws together with rules of customary ceremonial purity,[8] on the one hand, and in constant discourse, reflection, and controversy on the nature and implications of higher laws, of reason and conscience, namely, *dharma*, embodying rules and direction of right living, on the other. From one's understanding of *dharma*, one could challenge the laws of the state, customs and rituals, if one was prepared to invite the physical suffering which such a defiance would involve.

Such a provision – of claiming obedience to a higher moral law, in defiance of the state authority, inviting punishment and suffering on oneself for one's convictions, ennobling one's position and dramatising the conflict between oneself and one's rulers, and launching the strongest possible moral appeal for the change of position taken by authority – has been a living legacy in India. Mahatma Gandhi made the most effective use of such a legacy against the alien rule, and Jayaprakash Narayan used it against the excesses of the repressive indigenous rule of Indira Gandhi in the mid 1970s.

Unlike the growth of the assembly principle, which developed in Europe with the growth of guilds, parliaments, church councils, the Indian indigenous legislative experience remained too closely tied to canons and customs, giving enormous importance to kings and their advisers.[9] Moreover, the assembly principle, particularly for sharing political power, had a slim chance of developing in India because of constant invasions, conquests and social destabilisations, which enabled some of the most repressive regimes to go unchallenged.

What was developed, nevertheless, in the most enduring fashion, was the institution of *panchayat* (local council), embodying the theory and practice of the assembly principle at the grassroots level. These *panchayats* were manned by venerated village elders and enjoyed revenues and judicial and administrative powers of considerable importance. They survived, along with the village communities, through a succession of political regimes in Delhi and other regional capitals.[10]

The *panchayats* embodied the principle of decision-making in public matters by means of discussion and consensus. After the 1950s the Indian constitution revitalised and reconstituted them by means of one man one vote. Universal adult suffrage and enforced equality before law and in electoral politics, began radically altering political relationships in rural India. It supplied the much-needed provision for circumventing the firmly entrenched inequalities of the traditional social organisation.

The classical period of Indian civilisation thus has a continuing influence on her society and politics. Its manifold influence was neither totally replaced nor discarded by subsequent developments in her history. On the contrary, to some extent it provided the matrices which, along with other layers of her society, continued to exercise influence on her social and political life.

The Muslims started invading India, in numerous waves, from the eleventh century onwards, and by the time their rule finally disintegrated, under the Maratha and British attacks, they had been in India for more than eight centuries. During that period the Indians had experienced the ferocity of the Muslim sword, intolerance of any other religion, looting and plundering, on the one hand, and periods of enlightened administration, building activity and short-lived attempts to find out what other religions stood for, on the other. Under the monistic demands of Islam, reaching out to all forms of social activity, the capacity for tolerance on the part of Hinduism was stretched to its utmost. After centuries of Muslim bigotry, Hinduism emerged as a religion with a continued and renewed faith in tolerance so far as the bulk of its followers were concerned. In fact what helped it to survive was its deeply embedded philosophy of tolerance, relativism of truth, belief in the importance of man's inner experiences and, above all, inculcation of an ability to keep one's inner light burning even in the face of threats to one's physical existence.

Barring brief periods of enlightenment, under wise and just rulers, the scholars of Hinduism and Islam by and large maintained strict isolation. Whatever interpenetration of ideas, and limited appreciation of each other's point of view, did take place, was largely due to the herculean efforts of a few highly enlightened individuals, spread over centuries. In their encounter, Hinduism – a religion of the subject people during that period, with its own lack of organisation, a rigid caste system which condemned a section of its own people to socially low status, and without the facilities for proselytisation – suffered the most.

Given the nature of their encounter, and of the harsh historical reality of prolonged violence, one of the major emphases of Islam, on social equality, with significance for the hierarchically ordered Hindu social organisation, remained without much influence. The educated Hindu more readily accepted the message of social equality from the Western secular ideology of liberalism. The segment of Islam which enjoyed the respect of the Hindus was Sufism: like Hinduism, Sufism also emphasised relativism and tolerance.[11]

Subsequently, with the partition of India on supposedly religious lines, the fair treatment of the Muslims, together with the security of freedom of conscience, became a litmus test for Indian claims to secularity. Secularism, along with democracy, became the two cardinal principles of free India which enjoyed the implicit support of the entire spectrum of Indian political parties.

As a group, the Muslims of India have remained far more concerned with their freedom of conscience, cultural identity, physical safety and economic opportunities. And instead of using the democratic process of India to secure these by themselves, they often enter into clientilist deals with the Congress Party to provide them with all of these in return for their electoral support.

With *Pax Britannica,* the thinking men and women of India gained the much-needed opportunity to reflect on what had gone wrong with them as a people. They needed to take a hard look at some of the evil social practices which – owing to the indifference of the priestly and warrior castes, which continued to enjoy positions of power and influence, together with constant invasions and social dislocations – had received scant attention at their hands. Above all, what had made possible the prolonged period of social stagnation was the near absence of criticism of their social and political life. Intellectual vigour, the habit of discourse, criticism and the renewal of ideas on moral and philosophical issues, which were an integral part of culture, were now things of the past. In the rediscovery and revival of a corresponding spirit, the contact with the West, and Western education itself, were of inestimable value.

The revival of the 'spirit of criticism',[12] which was as much directed towards alien rule as towards some of the social practices, did not end the prolonged tradition of veneration for elders, superiors, teachers and rulers. Although the displacement of such a tradition has been woefully slow, nevertheless constructive criticism, criticism as fair comment, criticism in the public interest, criticism of the consequences of public policy, criticism to ensure continued creativity, etc., have increasingly gained legitimacy as a much-needed social practice.

The harsh comments of some of the arrogant colonial rulers, the claims to moral superiority made by Christian missionaries, and the growth of criticism and self-criticism, together stimulated the religious and social reform movements in India. In a highly segmented society, with its innumerable religions and caste groups, it was not easy to launch a unified reform movement. Consequently, a large number of religious and social reform leaders, over a period of nearly two centuries, began attacking evil social practices and the fossilisation of religion, and did much to restore the pride of the Indians in their own cultural heritage.

Closely connected with these were the movements demanding constitutional reform and political independence. These movements made the Indians realise how very important were the fundamental laws of the land, the nature and composition of public institutions, and the role of both constitution and judiciary in protecting the citizen against political authority.

The movements for social and religious reforms, on the one hand, and constitutional reforms and political independence, on the other, both of them involving social and political mobilisation on a mass scale, have left behind a deep impression on the Indian political society. In the post-independence period the importance of mass mobilisation – for the purposes of specific political objectives, electoral support, demanding the implementation of professed policies, or seeking political accountability of those in public office – continued unabated. In that sense, those movements constituted yet another layer, of great political significance, in Indian political society. Even to this day, the effectiveness of mass movement in getting political response has not come into question. Even when such movements fail to get an adequate response, the nature and organisation of their mobilisation come in for criticism and not mass movements as instruments of politics.

In the field of law and politics, the British influence on India had been immeasurably great. Moreover, Britain, when she came in contact with India, was herself going through profound domestic changes. Such changes were stimulated by industrialism, constitutionalism and the ideas associated with the French Revolution. Consequently, the exposure to Britain, when she herself was caught in the vortex of rapid social change, was of far greater significance than is commonly recognised.[13]

One of the major components of the Indian national movement was that of lawyers and constitutional lawyers. During the period of that movement, which was spread over nearly 100 years, India produced three generations of brilliant constitutional lawyers who had deeply assimilated the spirit of liberalism and the nature of its legal and political institutions. When, after attaining their independence, the Indians gained the opportunity to make their own constitution, her constitutional lawyers drew heavily on their own learning and experiences of constitutional law and the representative institutions of the Anglo-Saxon countries. Instead of taking into account the associated living of traditional India, they brought the individual to centre stage, provided him with a list of fundamental rights, and then charged the courts with the responsibilities for protecting those rights. Such an innovation came directly into conflict with the norms of traditional hierarchical social organisation. The interaction between these two sets of norms, of equality and hierarchy, became a source, as we shall see later on, of profound and almost endless social change in India after independence.

Finally, the emphasis on government by expert and impartial bureaucrats, the independence of the judiciary, freedom of press and association, the constituting of political authority at various levels of government by means of the ballot box, supremacy of civilian rule over the military, all these – inspired by British rule in India and the consequent freedom movement – laid the foundation of a free and democratic India.

The liberal legal and political values and institutions deeply influenced the traditional society of India. Initially, interest in them was expressed by the leaders of the Indian national movement as a means of strengthening their demands for self-government. Subsequently, in the post-independence period, the elite used the arguments of political liberalism to fight the deeply entrenched social inequalities in India's traditional society. Moreover, liberalism as an ideology effectively meshed with the implications for equality in the Hindu belief system, though not with her hierarchically ordered social organisation. While religious and philosophical ideas showed profound concern for the dignity and well-being of the individual, the traditional social organisation restricted such concerns for the people of higher castes. Whatever was not extended to the lower castes was often explained away, and rationalised, with the help of the doctrine of past *karma* and its consequences in the present life. Consequently, to the educated and social change minded Indian, the ideology of liberalism provided the much-needed stimulus, institutional provision and opportunity for realising its goals through political process and thereby circumventing the disadvantages of a hierarchical social system.

In a sense, the emphasis on the individual in Western political liberalism struck a responsive chord in the educated Indian, because the belief system of Hinduism had already sensitised him to the importance of the individual and his inner experiences. At the other extreme, however, there was the emphasis on group compliance to the norms of various castes. Such a basic dichotomy, of emphasis on the individual, in the belief system, and on his conformity to the norms of his caste, within the social organisation, have led to an extreme form of individualism in some matters and unquestioned group compliance in others. To the educated Indian, mindless group compliance often appeared to be a greater evil than the extreme form of individualism. Consequently, they welcomed the reinforcement of the individual, of his rational choices, and of his search for alternate choices, as emphasised by political liberalism. It was their hope that out of the reduced influence of the social organisation, diminished to cultural essentials, a relatively freer individual would emerge who would then be able to involve himself in the newly launched democratic process by means of a mutual accommodation of interests and group activity which cut across traditional divisions. In post-independence India, it was their approach which won the day.

The Indian borrowing of modern ideas, the emulation of Western legal and political institutions and, above all, the interaction of these with the indigenous, have been the subject of a lively controversy among the students of social sciences. Louis Dumont has argued that the vitality of Indian spiritual and philosophical pursuits resulted in an immense diversity of perspectives and ideas. Such an indigenous diversity further resulted in a temper and genius for building syncretic theories. Such a syncretic capacity helped India to absorb the impact of British rule as yet another exercise in intellectual assimilation.[14] M. N. Srinivas saw limitations in Indian syncretic capacity and pointed out that at times an extraneous influence may remain confined to a specific area.[15] Milton Singer used the notion of the 'coexistence' of the indigenous and the borrowed to explain social change in those segments of society where syncretic assimilation on the indigenous side or absorption on the exogenous side did not take place.[16]

There is yet another way of looking at this phenomenon of what in fact happens to what has been borrowed from outside. While in a number of cases, there is spontaneous borrowing and effortless assimilation into the cultural base of society, there are also as many cases of unassimilated coexistence of the compatibles and incompatibles. The compatibles may coexist as they may not compete for exclusive support. The case of incompatibles is different. The incompatibles interact, interpenetrate and produce something different and unintended. The result of the interaction of each set of incompatibles can be identified by means of specific research and analysis. Consequently, any simplistic theory, either of Westernisation or syncretic assimilation, is likely to be misleading.

In this particular respect, nevertheless, the Indian intellectual heritage, from the days of her classical civilisation, has proved to be of lasting value. Her philosophical background by and large favoured plurality in thought, culture, religion and society. It also favoured the inclusion of the incompatibles within comprehensive intellectual, philosophical and social systems. In other words, Indian philosophical thought, instead of regarding the presence of contradictions as a mark of imperfect reasoning or condition, viewed it as a situation requiring special intellectual effort and categories in order to include and accommodate the differences in thought, religion and society.

In that respect, the course of Indian intellectual development was different from the rationalism of Western Europe, from Socrates to Immanuel Kant. To European thinkers, the presence of contradictions in reasoning was a mark of illogicality, imperfect argument and the lack of intellectual maturity in general. Later on, in the ideas of Hegel and Marx, contradictions came to play an important role as a necessary logical or social idiom through which a higher intellectual or social evolution became possible.

Indian philosophical thinking, however, couched some of its major ideas in terms of plurality, contradiction, coexistence and attainment or non-attainment of the state of higher unity.

Such a philosophical background gave rise to, and sustained, a social and intellectual culture whereby plurality, contradiction, coexistence were treated as characteristics of different aspects of reality to be reckoned with and accommodated, rather than ignored or explained away by means of neat intellectual arguments. Such a background also favoured the living of individual and social life in more than one single internally consistent, rationally ordered, intellectual or social system. Under the circumstances, the average citizen could make his living in a newly-developed urban industrial environment, follow religions and rituals which might have developed in the sixteenth century, subscribe to philosophical thought which developed

1000 years before Christ, and yet not experience the anguish of unliveable contradictions in one's life or of being pushed around in different directions. Such a background has also helped the Indians to live with ease within the framework of liberal political institutions borrowed from the West, with their own emphasis on individuality and equality, and their traditional social organisation with an undying emphasis on conformity and hierarchy. Unlike individuals in other societies, the Indians find themselves living out different aspects of their lives in cultural systems and their norms which had developed at different times in their long history, and still remain as much at ease with themselves as people in any other system.

The above argument suggests that the political society of India needs to be understood in relation to various historical phases, religions and cultural backgrounds, value emphases and, above all, intellectual systems which left behind a lasting influence on her people. References to them, in India's long history, became necessary in order to understand the peculiarities of the various patterns of social and political behaviour.

Through the Crucible of Democratic Process

Scant attention has been paid to the actualities of democratic process in India. Such actualities often go unnoticed because the corpus of theoretical knowledge available for interpreting them is itself deeply grounded in political experiences of a different kind and therefore remains insensitive to the peculiarities of political societies outside that region. Scholars equipped with such tools of knowledge seek to identify merely the parallels with Western political experience rather than to understand the actuals of political experience of a different sort.

Liberal political systems of the countries of the West have been products of specific economic and historical forces in the seventeenth to nineteenth centuries. These forces gradually refashioned legal and political institutions of the countries of Western Europe and North America so that they permitted certain forms of social and economic activity which are broadly associated with the term capitalism. The growth of capitalism itself, with which the emergence of liberal democracy in the West is associated, was indeed a complex phenomenon. And as Max Weber has reminded us, it is fallacious to assume that it simply emanated from the previous form of social and economic organisation, namely, feudalism. In its emergence, a number of historical forces converged, ranging from profit motive and efficient industrial and organisational means to realise it, thrift, reinvestment, religious justification of profit-seeking activity, urban class, objective laws, bureaucracy, rational bookkeeping, land tenure, new notions of individual rights and state authority, etc.

As opposed to that, the growth of democratic process in developing societies, wherever it exists, has largely been a product of movements for political independence from colonial rule, constitutional reforms, exposure to Western political ideals and institutions, the commitment of a political elite, direct or indirect support from indigenous beliefs and practices, increasing involvement in the political process, and above all learning to protect one's interests, and the interests of groups and the community, by means of such a process.

Consequently, within developing countries, the emergence of democratic process created problems which were materially different from their counterparts in the West. For one thing, in the former it created an interaction between the indigenous social organisation, based on the norms of hierarchy, and the new legal and political institutions, based on the norms of equality. It also created a problem for the traditional attitude to authority which was compliant rather than questioning. Above all, it created the need for the growth of political capacity to be able to make use of the new political process. Finally, the new political institutions, which were emulated from outside, required the learning and assimilation of the dos and don'ts of their own operation. Without such an assimilation of dos and don'ts, both normative and pragmatic, the survival of new institutions became precarious. In this section, we shall examine some of these and other related problems.

One of the basic problems which the newly introduced democratic institutions and practices had to face in India was the need to operate in a stratified social organisation with segmented cohesion within all its constituent caste groups. Such a cohesion also existed within religious groups and their subgroups. The traditional social organisation, based on rigid hierarchical lines, had been a part of India's culture and tradition for nearly three millennia. Such deeply entrenched social institutions, based on the norms of hierarchy, were lined up against new legal and political institutions and their claims to equality. Their encounter, which captured the imagination of scholars the world over, has been documented in various scholarly writings in the social sciences. Contrary to the pessimistic prediction of some of them,[17] the democratic process in India gradually started nibbling away at the social cohesion which, over the years, had extended itself from the various traditional concerns to non-traditional areas. Election after election registered greater and greater differentiation in the electoral choice of voters of the same caste.[10] Such an electoral differentiation was spearheaded by the upper castes, gradually followed by the rest. In some cases this was so despite efforts by campaigning politicians to turn their traditional cohesion into a 'vote bank' or to enter into clientilist vote bartering in return for economic advantage.[19]

So far as some of the traditional social institutions of caste groups were concerned, they began to roll themselves back to their primary social concerns of endogamy, ritual and pollution.

The presence of traditional social cohesion of various castes, and its encounter with the voter's need to make rational and secular choices, unencumbered by such a cohesion, did initially create a problem. In the course of time the splitting force of democratic process gained an edge over cohesion in non-traditional areas such as voting in elections. Such an encounter, and experience, has very few parallels. Some of the theoretical interpretations used to understand the Indian democratic experience, with the caste system in the centre of it, by means of perspectives and theories used in order to understand the political participation of various ethnic groups in the American democratic process, proved to be much less helpful.[20] Such interpretations have become telling illustrations of seeing parallels, in place of actuals, for which there was limited justification. The manner in which the democratic process made inroads into the extended cohesion of castes, and brought about a roll-back effect – so as to remain involved with the primary concerns of caste, namely, endogamy, ritual and pollution – has varied in different castes and regions. It therefore requires intensive and longitudinal studies of the shaping of the actualities of such a cohesion in its encounter with democratic process. Neither the parallels from Western experience nor the concept of social cohesion were of much help in this case.

For the operations of democratic institutions – based on the principle of one man one vote, electorally mandated authority, majority–minority decision-making mechanisms and, above all, questioning, criticising and seeking to replace those in elective public office, all unfamiliar to traditional ways of behaviour – the political society of India, especially at the grassroots level, had to undergo two signifi-

cant changes. They were: the bifurcation of social and political leadership; and change in political relationships, within and among various social groups, independently of their positions in the
hierarchically ordered traditional social organisation.[21] The
democratic process itself induced such changes.

The traditional leaders of rural India, where the bulk of her population lives, did not find the principle of one man one vote, majority
rule, open discussion and criticism, in short a questioning political
culture, to their liking. For centuries they were regarded as venerated leaders with high familial status of their own. The democratic
process, much to their dismay, brought into the elected bodies, and
in various discussion-cum-gossip groups, younger men who were not
always mindful of age or traditional social status when putting forward their own ideas or criticisms. Consequently, the older and
socially venerated leaders reluctantly handed over political leadership of their groups or villages to the younger men, often from the
same families or those with equivalent social standing, and retained
social leadership concerning traditional group matters in their own
hands. Such a bifurcation between the elders, continuing leadership
of their groups in traditional matters, and the younger men as political leaders, engaged in building a network of support structure across
the ethnic divide, in order to wield political power in a numerically-
based democratic system, demarcated jurisdictions for both.

Such a bifurcation also gave the younger leaders a freer hand to
operate in various public institutions with much less commitment
to those normative values which often restrained their elders.
Detached from the traditional normative constraints of their elders,
these younger men introduced an element of political flexibility and,
at times, cynical opportunism, into the pursuit and retention of political power. When some of the leaders of this generation entered state
assemblies and/or *loksabha* (parliament), they carried with them a
predilection for horse-trading and floor-crossing for office or cash,
and a lack of commitment in general, which often shocked their constituents. Not all who graduated through such a democratic process
in rural India displayed such political unreliability. Moreover, such
a political element also became increasingly vulnerable as competition for political power became more intense.

The other significant change which had occurred in traditional
society as a result of the introduction of democratic institutions and
procedures was that it provided the socially lower segments of society with an opportunity to circumvent, in law and in electoral poli

tics, the disadvantages which their traditionally lower status had imposed on them. In other words, the people of lower-middle and lower castes, who often constituted larger groups numerically speaking, were able, by means of the electoral process, to get into public bodies and control them. Through the democratic process, then, the traditionally lower segments of society were not only altering the nature of political relationships, between themselves and those socially above, but were also using such a process to force the pace of social change in general in a stubbornly unchanging society.

The democratic process, under the circumstances, served, and is serving, a much wider purpose in India than in most other political societies. For one thing it has just about become a potent instrument in the hands of those who were condemned to socially and economically disadvantageous positions for centuries. But such a process, as might be expected, is exploited and distorted at the hands of wiley politicians who promise one thing and actually do something else. Nevertheless, potentially such a process has every possibility of setting right deeply entrenched social inequalities. The democratic process in India thus serves a unique purpose, a purpose which is often lost sight of by theories of political development.

This then brings us to the core issue within the Indian democratic process itself. Unlike the countries of Western Europe and North America, democratic institutions in India, with universal adult suffrage, freedom of speech and association, fundamental rights and judicial protection of them, etc., were introduced in advance of a commensurate political capacity to be able to use them effectively. Consequently, these basic attributes of a democratic system remained as mere constitutional provisions for future use, until an adequate political capacity on the part of individuals could develop. Such a problem, of constitutional provisions provided in advance of the growth of the political capacity to use them effectively, did not arise in the countries of Western Europe and North America. That is because in those countries individual rights were conceded gradually, in instalments, and almost always in delayed response to prolonged demands for them. The political mobilisation in support of such demands, often spread over a long period, prepared the people well in advance for the enjoyment of those rights. Consequently, in the case of such countries the problem of the growth of individual political capacity in order to utilise those rights was not of the same magnitude.

This meant that such provisions, secured in advance, had to wait until the people matured politically and were able to appreciate and use them. In India, in particular, it has been a case of differentiated use of such provisions, as there are vast differences in the growth of individuals' political capacity. Those segments of society which had more education, economic resources, had come into contact with men in public office, and were prepared to involve themselves in the political process, were the first to take advantage of the various provisions of the constitution and public policy. Others, by means of emulation, mobilisation by interested politicians, or through their own gradual political involvement, learned to utilise such provisions to protect their interests.

Behind the growth of human political capacity to utilise various constitutional provisions, to protect one's interests and the interests of one's group, and, above all, to obtain response and accountability from those who are in public office, there is the universal problem of how people mature politically. Once again, India, with her unique problems of traditional social inequality, demonstrates a kind of experience of differentiated constraints, political distances, deeply ingrained fears of government *qua* government, etc., which hardly has a parallel.[22]

Then there is the problem of learning the dos and don'ts of operating liberal political institutions which were transplanted from elsewhere. Such dos and don'ts were rarely identified in scholarly writings and the knowledge of them was considered to be obtainable by means of actual political involvement. The successful working of liberal political institutions in countries such as Britain, the United States and France points to the presence of certain normative and pragmatic imperatives which have to be learned in order to ensure the survival of democratic institutions. These imperatives point out that for the people on either side of the political divide, there is a certain lesson to be learned, namely that liberal political institutions survive where the citizens are able to strike a balance between what is normatively desirable and what is politically possible. Excessive normative commitment, in the form of ideology, religion or personal morality, on the one hand, and overly pragmatically cynical political opportunism, on the other, do not provide conditions in which liberal political institutions can be sustained.

Political societies which aspire to sustain their liberal political institutions will have to develop their own widely-shared notions of what is fair and what is not fair in the political field. Such notions will also help the average individual to civilise an otherwise most competitive, and often ruthless, segment of human activity. They will have to emphasise also what is democratically proper or improper in the treatment of their political adversaries. Further, involvement in the democratic process cannot always rest on idealistic notions of public weal. What it therefore calls for is the formulation of notions which define propriety, both moral and legal, in the 'fit' between one's private interests and public interests. People join democratic politics for a variety of reasons: power, status, glory, indirect material gain and public service. In order to make the citizen's involvement in democratic politics more realistic and worldly, it is important that the notions of a proper 'fit' between public and private interests are widely discussed and shared. A situation where a moral hyperbole is used by those in power, leaving no ground for the scrutiny of their own public conduct, almost always provides a situation of abuse of such power.

The political elite of developing countries, which tried to borrow Western liberal political institutions and emulate the conduct of their public life in general, paid heavily for neglecting their unwritten dos and don'ts, which are never explicitly stated but which, nevertheless, act as the foundation of those institutions. Moreover, such notions of dos and don'ts, with their normative emphases, have to be related to one's own cultural experiences. For the developing countries, therefore, it is indeed a formidable undertaking to build a set of dos and don'ts of their own, with reference to their own cultural and ethical tradition, to act as a protective umbrella over their newly established liberal institutions.

So far as the Indian experience of building such normative as well as pragmatic imperatives is concerned, it points to an extraordinarily complex process of learning of a people. The problem of normative–pragmatic guidance was evolved with the help of what the indigenous religious and cultural traditions had emphasised, what the constitutional reform movement and the struggle for independence had underlined, and, above all, what was demonstrated through the political conduct of India's top-flight leaders before and after independence. In addition to what mattered was one's own notions of right and proper while one was actually involved in political situations. All these, together, made the Indian experience of learning the dos and don'ts of operating liberal political institutions a unique one.[23]

Conceptual Inadequacy

The Indian democratic experiment in a multilayered society, with adaptations and modifications of incredible complexity, has questioned some of the assumptions and the conceptual adequacy of political development theories which are based almost entirely on the historical experiences of a few Western countries. Some of these, which have come into question, are as follows:

(a) At the root of several versions of liberal and Marxist theories of development there is an underlying assumption that political institutions have grown in the way they have as a result of the shaping and determining influences of a prior social and economic development. While the liberal development theorists such as Max Weber and Karl de Schweinitz have argued in favour of the *convergence* of a large number of historical social forces, predominated by the economic, the Marxist theorists have attributed a near causal influence to the economic forces in producing the type of political organisation which comes into existence in any particular society.

As opposed to this assumption, at least in the initial years following independence from colonial rule, the developing countries of our time, through their nationalist political elite are, and were, able to exercise the choice, in most cases, as to the type of political institutions they wanted to have. The Indian nationalist leaders and constitutional lawyers – who, during the prolonged period of national movement spread over nearly 100 years, had deeply assimilated the significance of Anglo-Saxon liberal political ideology to their near stagnant social organisation and their deeply ingrained fear of government *per se* – had exercised *their* choice in having Westminster-style parliamentary democracy. In their case, it was an elite choice undictated by economic circumstances, dominant economic classes or international economic pressures.

Such an *initial* political choice, however, was also caught in the indigenous web of economic relationships which then began to use and influence it to their own advantage. The initial political choice, nevertheless, laid down the matrix within which the subsequent political development took place.

(b) The other assumption of political development theories which seems to lay itself open to question is the notion of participation. Historically speaking, the increasing volume of participation in public decision-making processes, as the experiences of Britain, the United States and France have suggested, had been one of the con-

cessions in grudging instalments made by people in power in response
to pressures of agitation and threats of revolution. As opposed to that
the Indians, right from the start, not only made provision in their
constitution for democratically-elected political authority in the centre and the states, but also extended that principle to the districts,
subdistricts and villages. Such comprehensive participatory measures were introduced because of the idealism and vision of India's
nationalist political elite, which came to power when colonial rule
ended, rather than by means of political pressure generated from
below as was the case in Western countries.

The provision for public participation in India, in a socially unequal and hierarchically arranged traditional society, created peculiar
problems of its own. As everywhere else, the economically better off
and socially higher up got much more, initially, out of such provisions. Their social and economic background helped them to become
the initial users of such provisions. Nevertheless, the very presence
of such provisions, increasingly brought into the political process –
as a result of emulation, envy and growing awareness that through
participation in the deliberations of public bodies, which made decisions affecting everyone, one would be better able to protect and serve
one's individual and group interests – those who were a few steps
behind the initial users. Those social groups which were at the bot-
tom of the social hierarchy, and which had attributed their own lower
positions to their past *karma* or god's will, took the longest to explore
the provisions of participation. Their use of such provisions was also
mediated and bartered by a political elite which wanted their numer-
ical support in return for questionable promises.

Unlike Western democracy, therefore, the problem of political participation was not one of absence of its provision but of individual
political capacity to be able to use it without being duped by political middlemen.

(c) The various models used in the explanation of party organisations, which are also based almost entirely on their growth and
experiences in a handful of Western countries, often fail to identify
the peculiarities of such organisations in the non-Western societies.
What such models seem to take far too seriously is the activities of
party organisations at the time of elections and the nature of the support structure they build in order to win elections. What those models
ignore, therefore, is what happens to those support structures at various levels below party officials and party elected deputies. At those
levels, the behaviour of individuals supporting competing party struc-

tures tends to ignore, and transgress, the artificial political cleavages and divisions set up by party organisations to conduct their electoral politics. Such cleavages dissolve much sooner in developing countries than in the developed. The rhetorical and theatred conflict of electoral politics, based on a shifting mosaic of support structures, is often unable to hold competing groups, as identifiable adversaries, long after an election. Despite strenuous efforts by party organisers, strange and sometimes unbelievable accommodations and combinations develop across party lines and at various levels of party membership.

For the purposes of election, party organisers who venture beyond primary groups for electoral support build support structures which cut across ethnic, religious and regional ties. However, their supporters often do not wish to remain in a state of perpetual conflict, even if it is a rhetorical and artificial conflict, with the members of their own primary groups. Consequently, soon after an electoral contest, they start talking across the party fence and make a mockery of the party and electoral divisions. In other words, the phenomenon of associated living, within groups to which one is born, provides a process which is the very reverse of electoral strife, particularly in developing countries.[24]

Party organisations in developing countries, including India, operate in an environment of ephemeral support, quick dissolutions and stranger-than-fiction combinations. And there are hardly any theoretical models which recognise the *presence* of such a phenomenon, let alone help us examine it.

There is yet another problem with concepts of party organisation largely formulated to examine the experiences of Western countries. Such concepts often fail to identify party-like substitutes or pre-party political entities in developing countries. But what is more, such concepts often fail to identify the fairly widespread phenomenon of mass movement–party–mass movement cycle in developing countries.

In the post-independence period, the overarching national movement, embracing so many interests, turns into a ruling party. It then creates factions of dissatisfied people within its ranks who mobilise support for their own causes. In that process they either build rival parties of their own or go into the political wilderness. In either case, they wait for the ruling party to lose its support and then launch a mass movement, by temporarily joining similarly dissatisfied political elements, capture power, once again become a ruling party, and set in motion yet another round of the mass movement–party–mass movement cycle.

India, in particular, has gone through this cycle and there is no knowing when it will end. The Indian National Movement, a mass movement, was followed by the rule of the Congress Party, leading to its displacement at the hands of the Janata movement in 1977, which in turn was displaced by a rival movement launched by Indira Gandhi in 1980.[25]

(d) The concept of class, and its use, represents an interesting illustration of looking for parallels, in place of actuals, in the social and political analysis of developing countries. Karl Marx had elevated the term class to an extremely significant concept of social analysis. Despite the constant use of this concept to explain class formations, class determination of the realities of social organisation and class conflict as a necessary conduit for social evolution, Marx could not devote an exclusive work of his own for an extended treatment of this concept as he had earlier planned.[26] After Marx, the concept of class, as he understood it, became a subject of many interpretations.[27] The boldest among these was Dahrendorf's *Class and Class Conflict in Industrial Society*. In that work he argued that to Marx, the concept of class was not a means of understanding social stratification but 'a tool for the exploitation of changes in total societies'.[28] In other words, the concept of class had become as much political as economic and, what is more, an indispensable key to understanding social changes in history.

Marx had used the concept of class to understand the nature of social change in European social and economic organisation since the days of classical antiquity, through feudalism, to the growth of industrial capitalism. He had, however, avoided a detailed analysis of agricultural societies such as the Indian and Chinese because, in his view, they had 'no known history',[29] as compared to the evolution of industrialised societies. And so far as India was concerned, Marx had hoped that the British rule would sweep away the vertical divisions of caste and the horizontal divisions of village sentiment; after that, the undivided masses would be able to generate their own political effectiveness for social change on the lines suggested by the history of industrialised societies. The Indian political society, needless to say, did not develop on those lines. Caste system and village sentiment remained intact when British rule ended, and despite their divisions they generated effective political pressure to gain independence.

At the other extreme, the concept of class as a tool of identifying social stratification did not help very much either so far as the Indian situation was concerned. For there is essentially a duality of class in India: the class to which one is born through one's caste, and class as an occupational and income category. One may be able to change the latter by means of education, new skills and mobility. There is, however, a class reference implicit in a caste system which, apart from its hierarchical element, also refers to caste-bestowed occupation. The occupational reference in the caste system exercises a powerful influence on the minds of men. The ex-untouchables of India often refer to it in the language of *karmic* predetermination by the lord almighty. Very few, therefore, are able to move out of such an occupational reference. Consequently, to use the concept of class independently of caste, either for the purposes of social stratification or for its potential for political action, does not help very much in understanding the Indian situation. Such a situation, in fact, calls for its own analysis of social change with the help of concepts which explain the actualities of India's social life rather than with the help of assumed parallels with social situations elsewhere.

(e) The repeated attempts by some of the developing countries since attaining their independence to introduce and reintroduce a representative form of government in the face of repeated takeovers by the army, has sensitised scholars to the problem of political instability and its links with factors other than the army.

Some of the broader definitions of political instability – as essentially a problem of the developing countries, as opposed to the democratic structures of Western countries, which are inviolate, unbreached and unassailable – are giving way to the need to identify those forces which, from time to time, undermine the political stability even of Western countries. While military takeovers in some Western countries may have become a thing of the past, periodically, nevertheless, a number of forces do undermine the representative character of their political societies, causing political instability, though not of the ultimate degree. Crises in foreign policy (in Britain during the Suez crisis, in the United States during the Vietnam War and in France during the Algerian crisis), defence policy, powerful business, industrial and union lobbies subverting the electoral mandate, the media shifting the locus of political discussion from human assembly to electronic communication, etc., have together made significant infractions into the democratic process of Western countries. While such infractions are potentially present in all political societies, it is the military infraction of democratic civilian rule which receives maximum attention.

In the absence of the means, experience and tradition with which to fight back against infractions, through public criticism, political agitation, effective use of electoral machinery to reflect shifts of opinion and, above all, fiercely independent public men and judiciary, the developing countries do not as yet get many chances to restore resilience and mend their democratic fences. Nevertheless, through widespread protests, the expression of critical public opinion, the internalisation of the need for political opposition, and agitation bordering on violence, they have increasingly exerted more pressure against those forces which have sought to constrain their public institutions.

The infraction–resilience approach to democratic process, and to the consequent problem of political instability, does not regard democracies as inviolate anywhere. On the contrary, it shifts our attention to the effective uses of resilience processes, in the face of infractions, in politically mature societies.

Our increasing understanding of such processes, and of the potential danger of political instability in all political societies, makes us take a hard look at the assumptions of political development theory which treat such a problem as a problem only of developing countries.

For infractions against their own democratic institutions, particularly during the 1970s, the Indians were able to draw upon their experiences of non-violent political resistance. By means of moral and philosophic ideas on *satyagrahic* non-violent resistance, and its continual demonstration in practice in rural and urban India, Mahatma Gandhi left behind a rich legacy of political resistance. Such a legacy, of resistance against alien rule, was later on extended against the excesses of indigenous rule by Jayaprakash Narayan.

The theory and practice of political resistance is, therefore, deeply ingrained in the Indian political psyche. People opposed to political authority or public policy keep toying with the idea of making use of it in rural as well as urban India. Consequently, even in the examination of political resistance offered by India's people, we have to take into account the actualities of the uses of her own heritage of resistance against authority.

Looking at some of the complexities of India's multilayered political society, and the equally complex adaptations and accommodations brought about in her social and political life as a result of her involvement in democratic process, one is inclined to conclude that she

represents a formidable challenge to our theoretical capacity to interpret and explain the nature of her political development. While our
concepts and theories grow in their capacity to undertake a task of
such an enormity, what we can do, to begin with, is to know more
about the actualities of her development processes in specific areas
rather than reach out to them, speculatively, as parallels of
experiences elsewhere.

II CHINA

China is another major non-Western multilayered political society.
Towards the understanding of her social change, a number of sweep-
ing generalisations have been made, ranging from 'the unchanging
east' to a total change in her traditional social and political life under
Maoist Cultural Revolution.[30] The complexity of gradual change,
which took place before the revolution, and has continued since then,
has been effectively identified by those scholars who view the
phenomenon of change as an integral part of the society–polity con-
tinuum rather than by those who are given to building abstract
theoretical formulations first of all, largely based on the experiences
of a select number of Western countries, and then perceiving, interpreting and explaining change through the assumptions of such formulations. In this section we shall therefore concentrate on some of
those explanations which see the nature and extent of social change
as an integral part of the ongoing social and political process within
a multilayered political society which has been there for centuries.
To be able to identify the actualities of social change since the revolution, we have to steer clear of the two mutually exclusive assumptions of no change and total change in China's political society.[31]

The Multilayered Political Society of China

The multilayered political society of China, with a baffling number
of layers in it, is one of the oldest in the world. These layers, as in
any other continuing civilisation, exercise their own influence. One
of the most significant of such layers, and perhaps of lasting influence,
is what is known as the age of Chinese philosophers and classics. During that period, ranging roughly from 722 to 481 B.C., China registered an extraordinary range of philosophical activity to which a large

number of social and political questions, along with their ethical connotations, were raised, discussed and recorded by the disciples of her great scholars. One of these, Confucius, had a profound influence on Chinese society, politics and ethics. He viewed the problem of government essentially from the perspective of ethics and emphasised the need for rulers to set a good example by means of their own conduct. In other words, he brought the conduct of rulers within the framework of moral obligation. He also urged his people, in order to avoid conflict, to discover and act within their own 'assigned roles'. Within the relationships between the ruler and the ruled, he maintained, state functionaries had an enormous role to play. In order to humanise the exercise of power, he wanted that class to cultivate the virtues of inner integrity, righteousness, loyalty, reciprocity and, above all, to show genuine human consideration. Over and above these inner virtues, they were also expected to cultivate the *'li'*, or a sense of propriety and fairness.[32] His prescriptive humanism, particularly for those who were involved in the business of governance, had a lasting effect on Chinese tradition and culture.

Although Confucianism and its subsequent interpretations exercised an enormous influence on the social and political life of China, it was by no means the only influence. Some of the equally powerful influences were from the School of Legalism, requiring strict enforcement of laws and sound bureaucratic control of society, and Taoism, which emphasised a withdrawal and an inactive approach on the part of the rulers, especially in the day-to-day life of subjects. Then there was the Han Confucianist approach, which emphasised the importance of moral persuasion, without undermining the importance of law. Such emphases deeply influenced Confucian scholars, who joined state bureaucracy in large numbers and brought the importance of principles that were implicit in them to bear on their functions as employees of the state.[33] During China's long history, this body of principles and administrative precepts acquired several reinterpretations and reformulations.

Under Buddhism, and in the subsequent neo-Confucianism in particular, the dual framework of earlier Confucianism – emphasising obligations on both sides of human relationships, i.e. king–subject, husband–wife, master–servant, etc. – gave a relatively greater importance to the stronger element within those relationships. In the political field this meant autocracy. Consequently, despite the rich heritage of philosophical principles and prescriptions for humanising administrative and political relationships, Chinese political society, over a prolonged period, continued to be governed by a different degree of autocracy.

In recent times, particularly in the nineteenth century, when Chinese scholars began to take the liberal political traditions of the West seriously, their own prolonged tradition of political autocracy made any liberalisation of the regime an impossibility. Unlike India, which also underwent a lengthy experience of political autocracy, but nevertheless embarked on a prolonged national movement for self-government and civil rights, and thereby registered a break from the past, China's resistance to foreign invasion, with a few exceptions, was launched by men in military uniform. For a long time China had believed in her own supremacy in spiritual matters. So far as the intellectual ferment of the mid-nineteenth century and the demand for social and political reform were concerned, they proved ineffective. Such demands, moreover, could not by themselves provide a vision of the future. This was also true of highly dedicated leaders like Sun Yat-Sen. Later on, Mao Tse-tung filled that vacuum and provided both a vision of the future and a sense of direction on Communist lines.[34]

Despite some of the earnest efforts made by reform-minded Chinese intellectuals in the nineteenth and early twentieth centuries who had come under the influence of Western political ideals, the layer of Western liberalism on the Chinese political society remained far too ineffective. When Confucianism, which had undergirded the cohesiveness of Chinese political society with its principles and prescriptions for government and administration for centuries, began to crumble, its place could not be taken by a Chinese version of West-influenced liberalism. What followed was a competition between the alien ideologies of Christianity, Republicanism, Social Darwinism and, above all, Marxism–Leninism, together with an intense military conflict.[35] In such a competition what won out was the Maoist form of Marxism with its ability to mobilise a large number of people, rebuild the cohesion of China's political society, all with the help of norms and institutions of an ideology which came from outside. Such norms and institutions inevitably interacted with those of the traditional Chinese society, changing that society, and in the process themselves undergoing change.

One of the central emphases of Confucian theory, which constituted an ideal of Chinese society for centuries but was not realised in practice, was that of social equality. Confucius had argued that while human beings in their native make-up were unequal, education should become the means of narrowing down inequality.

Simultaneously, he also emphasised the merit system to recognise the social importance of those who made a greater contribution to society. The Chinese Communists, while officially upholding Marxian ideology, came out with the most effective expression of a homegrown and deeply assimilated notion of social equality in their official pronouncements.[36] So while economic and political institutions, rooted in Confucianism, were replaced by Maoism, some of its normative emphases, very much a part of Chinese moral and social fabric, continued to be expressed in a mixture of old and new principles.

Mao's ideology, despite its Marxian inspiration and source, was deeply rooted in his *own* experiences leading the guerrilla movement in Yenan, mobilising landless peasants, military encounters with the Japanese and Chiang Kai-shekh armies, and above all a pragmatic groping as to what will and will not work, given the conditions of China. There was yet another 'given' in the situation which he was required to tackle, namely the deeply entrenched traditional social organisation based on the teachings of Confucius. In Mao's ideas, policies and strategies, therefore, there was a great awareness of all these components of the situation.

While Mao could easily identify the bureaucracy and the landed interests of the preceding period, he had a colossal problem getting at the traditional social system based on a network of kinship ties.[37] In a sense, Mao's Cultural Revolution, which was a criticism both of the traditional society and the manner in which the Communist political system operated within it, was an expression of his desperation to force the pace of social change which had run into unforeseen obstacles.

The interaction between the norms of harmony and reciprocity in the traditional social organisation, and those of conflict and the dictatorship of the workingman in the new ideology, had its own consequences for the network of social and political relationships. Since very little social science field research is permitted in China, it is difficult to determine the exact consequence of such an interaction.

Scholars have tried to point out how the well-prepared schemes of highly motivated and disciplined Communist leaders got bogged down in the sea of the traditional ways of doing things.[38] In the traditional Chinese society, the administrative elite, despite the political distance between it and those it governed, operated in a more personal and persuasive manner, which in turn also exposed it to influences from the people. The prolonged durability of the administrative system of the past was partly ensured by the fact that in the actual implementation of policies and laws, the points of view, interests and pressures from the base were also taken into account. Such an administrative behaviour, which was deeply rooted in society, often made a considerable difference to the style of operation, and sometimes to the content, of policies. A similar adjustment became necessary in the case of the new administration under Mao. In their actual operation, the various new institutions came to acquire the characteristics of Chinese administration as such which had been there for centuries.

The interrupted conformity of the Chinese political society made any fundamental transformation within it extremely difficult, in a short period. The concentration of economic power, and its consequent influence, was relatively easier to deal with than the reshaping of the network of social relationships with their implicit norms of reciprocity, humanity and attitude to authority in general. Mao nevertheless sought to change them by bringing in the powerful trinity of government, party and army to his assistance. In the absence of field research reports, it is difficult to assess the extent of his success in this respect. Officially speaking, the birth of a new society, based on workers, peasants, progressive bourgeoisie, students and army, was announced. They were then expected to work across the traditional divide of kinship and operationally make such a new society a reality.[39]

Crucial to the nature of social change in Chinese society under Communism was the question of changes in her kinship system itself. According to some Chinese scholars, in the past, as also under Communism, one could switch sides with reference to how a particular public policy would affect one's family and kingroup.[40] Even within the Chinese bureaucracy, the lower echelon looked to the upper in essentially kinship or kinship–parallel terms. Individuals in the upper echelons were referred to as elder brothers, uncles or teachers. Thus within the bureaucracy, as in society, 'pseudo-kinship' ties were created, where none had existed, so as to ensure mutuality of interests and protection. One's loyalty and moral obligation were coextensive with such groups.[41]

Kinship structure and its determining influence on individual and social conduct are deeply rooted in Chinese culture. They were also responsible for giving Chinese society what has appropriately been called 'negative stability' and minimal change. Throughout Chinese history, the bulk of her people remained busy with the interests of their families and kingroups, leaving the problem of government and the general direction of public policy to a small elite who had the inclination, training and ambition for them. At the root of China's prolonged stability, therefore, there was her kinship organisation, and the attitudes and behaviour patterns which it shaped. Mao was aware of the strength of such an organisation throughout Chinese history, but he had hoped that by preparing the younger generation, by means of ritual denunciation and public disassociation of the ways of elders, he might be able to limit its influence.[42]

Apart from the widespread organisation of kinship in China, there is also the presence of a number of nationalities where, for reasons of resistance to absorption in the larger Han community, there is a natural tendency to hold on to one's kinship ties.

China has a large number of nationalities or ethnic minorities. The largest group, namely, the Hans, constitute nearly 94 per cent of the population. In the remaining 6 per cent, there are nearly 56 minorities.[43] And in their resistance to absorption in the Han community, their kinship organisation has played an effective role. But what is more, since the *process* of social change in each of them is different, they do not respond to uniform, cut-and-dried solutions for their social development. They tend to follow a course of their own, despite several attempts to evoke a uniform response to a common nation-wide social stimulus. Very little, however, is known about their differentiated responses to a uniform attempt at inducing social change.

Political Process

Although the inspiration for Communism in China came both from Marxism and the Russian Revolution, Mao and his revolutionary associates depended far more on their own assessment of the revolutionary potential of different segments of their own society. Mao saw such a potential in China's landless peasantry which, in the eyes of orthodox Marxists, was a heresy. Since there was a limited working class in China, Mao did not want to wait until China expanded itself industrially and then organise her vastly expanded proletariat for a revolutionary assault. Moreover, the kind of class conflict which Marx had visualised between the bourgeoisie and the proletariat in an industrial society had its parallel, according to Mao, in the agricultural society of China, where a similar intensity of class conflict existed between the landowners and landless peasants. Consequently, by successfully mobilising the landless peasantry for the revolution, Mao had in fact short-circuited the various phases prescribed by the Marxists.

Maoist Communism, in other words, adapted the Marxian body of ideas, together with their various strategies, to suit Chinese historical and social conditions. While Mao had initially spurned the 'purity' of Marxism and its universal applicability, in the two major movements subsequently launched by him, i.e. the Great Leap Forward of 1958–59, and the Cultural Revolution of 1965–66, he had, to some extent, gone back to it. In launching both these movements, which had disastrous consequences, Mao had become a doctrinaire Marxist losing sight of the actualities of Chinese conditions. Moreover, in both cases, the party functionaries and bureaucracy[44] had shown much greater understanding of Chinese realities but had, reluctantly, gone along with the leader. Their opposition to Mao surfaced vehemently, in the form of a pragmatic reversal of his policies, after his death.

Being an old civilisation, with nearly 3000 years of recorded history, the Chinese did not take seriously either Marxism or modernism, both European in origin, and instead sought their own approaches and rationale to launch something that was parallel but homegrown. Even in the past, when China was confronted by a body of ideas from outside, she weighed them carefully in terms of their 'justification, equivalence, . . . congruence, . . . and absorption'.[45] Throughout the nineteenth and early twentieth centuries, Chinese scholars, before making a body of ideas from abroad known to their own people, weighed them in terms of their 'compatibility and complementarity' with the indigenous.[46]

A similar process seems to have been followed by Mao and his associates, in their selective borrowing from Marxism. Sometimes they even cited parallels between the Chinese and Marxian concepts. But such an exercise in parallelism, because of the basic differences between the two, did not go very far. The notion of ideology, for instance, remained foreign to the Chinese experience and therefore had to be equated to something that was closest, namely 'culture'. But what was more, Marxism, Chinese style, was expected to perform a comprehensive function similar to one performed earlier by Confucianism. In the words of a perceptive Chinese scholar, 'Communist ideology has replaced the Confucian *li*; it has taken over the latter's function as the culmination of what we in the West term social conscience, morality, religious faith, and constitutional law.'[47]

In the West, philosophical works, church, and finally a systematic body of law produced independent normative and legal systems over the years. As opposed to that, the traditional Chinese social system had put far greater emphasis on the internalisation of norms of behaviour rather than on overt compliance only. The traditional system in China, therefore, put a premium on self-discipline and self-direction after deeply assimilating the Confucian rules of right living.[48] In that sense its emphasis was similar to what Aristotle called law-abidingness as a more advanced state of social existence than merely having laws.

So far as Maoist Communism was concerned, it brought into play both the external system and the internalisation of its normative structure. In that sense something was added on to the traditional social system. Undoubtedly, an external system of laws had existed in the past. But the individual's conduct was moulded much more by the precepts of the elders, various teachings of Confucianism, and by compliance to group mores. To that were added the norms of the new social system. Like the norms of the traditional system, the new norms were expected to be deeply assimilated by the people. But infraction of the new norms met not merely with social disapproval but also with legal action.

Historically speaking, China was governed by means of a distant, but well-linked, state. Between China's far-flung, multilayered and complex society, on the one hand, and the bureaucrats, on the other, many forms of contact, operative links and styles of administration, embodying her traditional social philosophies, developed. On the top of these came Maoist Communism with its own sense of urgency towards a specific social direction. To that end it began using its three principal structural instruments: state or bureaucracy; party; and the army. As long as the intensity of the thrust of Maoist Communism continued, it correspondingly diminished the area of self-compliance and voluntarism in society. Once such a thrust began to lose its dynamism, the people at the receiving end of administration began to make their reaction to various policies known. Such reactions were expressed symbolically, indirectly, and always within the safe precincts of the winds of change. These, together, stimulated new stirrings within the realm of society. The people now could be openly critical of the policies of the Cultural Revolution.

Despite such a revival of the society of China, it is unthinkable that after nearly four decades of Maoist-style state intervention, she would ever go back to the pre-revolutionary state–society relationship. Too much had happened within the society itself during those decades of Maoism. And the Maoist-style, detailed and tightly controlled management of society may leave behind yet another layer of experience on her multilayered society. Nevertheless, in specific areas certain forms of social conduct and social values may register a comeback with a search for a more pragmatic approach to development.[49]

The political process within Chinese society is shaped and influenced by the normative deposits of her several layers of civilisation, the policies of the government of the day, the nature of actual decision-making as opposed to formal pronouncements, subtleties of symbolic expressions, an effective masking of one's political position within the framework of what is safe or not safe, and, above all, the intuitive capacity to detect at an early stage which of the competing sides would win out and then join it in time to gain advantage. All of this requires intensive, longitudinal and highly specific political study before one can be certain as to the nature of such a process.[50]

The political process of contemporary China, given her awesome complexities, can be studied neither solely in terms of her tradition and culture nor in terms of the radical changes which Mao sought to introduce. Least of all can it be studied solely by means of theoretical formulations which are deeply rooted in the political experiences of a few Western countries. Only after intensive and longitudinal field researches in various areas of her society and politics, if and when those are permitted, and with refinements and reformulations of the theoretical structures used for such research, will we have a more reliable knowledge of her political process. Until then our knowledge of it will remain indirect, sketchy, speculative and unsatisfactory.

Conceptual Inadequacy

China, like India, represents a major illustration of the impossibility of studying a non-Western political society in dichotomous, and mutually exclusive, tradition–modernity terms. As we saw in this section, China, a multilayered political society, has her own cultural legacies which are very much a part of her living present, and any conceptual approach which is premised on the assumption of her total break from the past – by means of a modernising Western ideology such as Communism, with its own apparatus of party bureaucracy and army – fails to take into account the social contexts within which her new institutions and procedures operate. Like political institutions and their operations anywhere in the world, those introduced in China under Communism are also context-dependent.

Moreover, the norms of these institutions interact with the norms of traditional society which have been there for centuries and have been too slow to change. What one needs to know, after painstaking field research, and not merely guesswork with the help of speculative theories, is the nature and extent of change in human social and political relationships which has, in fact, occurred as a result of such an interaction. While opportunities for such research are slow to come by, we can nevertheless say that the dichotomous concepts of tradition and modernity, which are viewed critically throughout this book, are woefully inadequate.

Equally unhelpful are those specific conceptual terms which, although deeply rooted in Western social and political experiences, are used to explain the social and political reality of China. The case in point here is Franz Schurmann's use of the terms 'organization' (as goal-oriented and well-disciplined) and 'institution' (as an integral part of social relationships).[51] Such highly specific meanings attached to two concepts do not enhance our understanding of one of the most complex political societies in the world. What such a use does, in effect, is to restrict our perspective and understanding within the arbitrary limits which the author prescribes to those two concepts. Moreover, by making use of such concepts, entirely derived from their use in explaining a Western social and political experience, we orient ourselves, from the start, to finding parallels with Western experiences elsewhere in the world. Under the circumstances, what gets overlooked are the actualities of those social and political experiences which might be different from our antecedent Western experience and which, therefore, may require new conceptual tools to examine them.

Ever since expatriate Chinese–American scholars pointed out, in the late 1960s, how much the Chinese political process is an integral part of the ongoing social process, to which the Communist ideology has made a significant but limited difference, students of Chinese society and politics have started taking the persisting, complex and subtle influences of Chinese cultural legacies seriously. Nevertheless, within the subdiscipline of political development, we are a long way

away from evolving conceptual tools to enable us adequately to analyse the complex mix of such a social and political process.

III JAPAN

Group Cohesion

Unlike the countries of Britain, the United States and France, where
the thrust of economic development was launched largely by the
entrepreneurial class, and which was spread over two to three centuries – and which simultaneously induced, and forced, a corresponding change in their legal and political institutions – the economic
development of Japan was a function of the decision and effort of
her ruling political elite, namely, the *samurais*. They, an elite group,
launched a movement towards Japan's economic modernisation with
all the vigour and effectiveness they could summon, and because of
them the Japanese attempt at industrialising was dubbed by scholars as 'Japan's Aristocratic Revolution'.[52]
    In that respect, Japan's situation was similar to Germany's, where
Prussian *junkers*, rather than the entrepreneurial class, industrialised
Germany in the initial period. Veblen and Bendix, as we saw earlier,
identified this as a different kind of industrial development with
different kinds of consequences on their legal and political institutions. Schumpeter, as we also saw earlier, reminded us that both Germany and Japan, under the circumstances, retained a large number
of characteristics of their pre-industrial societies. Since in their cases
industrialisation was both parachuted from above and accelerated,
neither country experienced the kind of social change which Britain, the United States and France did. Social change in Germany
and Japan was the result of the interaction of a borrowed technology and indigenous social organisation. As such, the consequence
of such a change was the enhancement of power of certain classes
with minimal changes in human social and political relationships.
    Due to the reductionist fallacies which, as we saw earlier, reduce
societies to industrialised or non-industrialised, regardless of what
else there is, and also due to the state of the social sciences, which
has a much greater degree of sensitivity to what exists in the West
or is similar to it, the peculiarities of Japan's political society were
often described in undifferentiating conceptual terms.
    The Japanese earned the unenviable title of 'the greatest borrowers'

at the hands of scholars and industrialists. Consequently, even when Japan came of age, technologically, the stereotype of her as 'the borrower' persisted. And what was worse, Japan was not seen as a select borrower, but as a total borrower who could do nothing on her own and retain nothing from her own past. In characterising Japan in that particular manner, what was left out was the need to identify Japan's subtle and select borrowing from Western sources, and her ability to incorporate it into an antecedent social organisation.

When Japan's technological and managerial performance began overtaking the Western world, the question raised by scholars as well as journalists, this time around, was what the West could borrow from Japan.[53]

There has been a belief amongst scholars that Japan, in the course of a little over a century, has been able to restructure all of her traditional institutions.[54] A conscious attempt was no doubt made, first by the Japanese themselves, and second by the Allied Occupation forces, to change as many of her traditional institutions as possible. Nevertheless, what needs to be identified is the nature and extent of change and, above all, the persistence of those social and cultural values which continued to influence and shape the working of new and transplanted institutions.

This then brings us to the question of group cohesion and cohesion within the society as a whole. Scholarly writings on Japan have yet to tell us about the why and how of her group cohesion. Quite often, instead of explaining the nature of cohesion in that society, attempts are made to compare it with the cohesion of society in feudal Europe or in small New England communities in the eighteenth century. And since the Western countries, after such an experience of cohesion, went through a period of individualism, Japan, it is often presumed, will also replicate such a course of development. Thus attempts to understand the peculiarities of Japanese cohesion are always cast in terms of a parallel and antecedent Western experience.

As examples of cohesion and consequent cooperation in Japan, the relationship between senior civil servants, on the one hand, and politicians, industrial houses and the elite in general, on the other, is often cited. Cooperation among them takes place within the framework of cultural traditions of a mutuality of interests, respect, trust and keenness jointly to find solutions to problems. Such traditions enable decision-makers to create an atmosphere of inclusiveness whereby nobody seems to be left out.

Such a shared sense of having been a party to the decisions made, and a self-assurance that one's interests are looked after as much as those of others, go beyond the capacity of existing conceptual knowledge to explain. The kind of cooperation from its constituents which an average society receives during an emergency, Japan seems to get at all times and at all levels of her decision-making process.

The peculiar nature of cohesion in Japanese society, before and after decisions are taken, seems to be at the centre of her social organisation, economy, polity, in short, in her decision-making process as such. What we need, therefore, is a theory of cohesion which can explain the essential nature of social togetherness, Japanese style, and not one that sees her cohesion as a parallel of what happened in feudal Europe.

Along with the peculiar nature of her cohesion, we also need to explain why a society, which is often dubbed as a 'borrower' society, which absorbs so many ideas from outside, does not allow her own roots to be shaken by what is incorporated. Even the uneven borrowing by different segments of her society, which should normally create situations of friction and rootlessness, as in other 'borrower' societies, leaves her essential cohesion undisturbed. The Japanese cohesiveness in the face of such borrowings must constitute a unique feat of not only incorporation but also balance. To date, scholars have merely admired it but have been unable to come up with theoretical tools to analyse and explain it.

The absence of marked individualism in Japanese political society has been attributed to certain traditional factors. One of them was that during the Tokugawa period in Japanese history, the 'ethic which stressed dependence' was emphasised. According to this explanation, 'vertical relations of dependence' were carefully emphasised and cultivated.[55] Thus the citizen depended on the emperor, pupil on teacher, servant on master, and so forth. By virtue of such ties, one did not face one's problems alone. Such a relationship, it was argued, continued even after the introduction of industry.

On the side of sanctions, Ruth Benedict argued that as opposed to the *guilt-culture* of industrial societies, Japan produced what she called a *shame-culture*. And despite industrialisation and urbanisation, 'personal submission' has remained as important in relationships as 'group identification'.[56]

What the Japanese did not develop, despite their industrialisation and urbanisation, was the kind of post-feudal economic and political individualism, or 'individuation' as Dore called it, which was developed by political societies of Western Europe. And if there was any individualism in Japanese society, it was by default, as Marion Levy observed with reference to Chinese society, rather than a product of a philosophical principle.

Thus Benedict, Dore and Levy put an enormous emphasis on a kind of individualism which is associated with commercial and industrial capitalism, and with political liberalism in a few Western countries. Instead of explaining its absence, in historical and contextual terms, they saw it as a serious shortcoming in Japanese political society. In their view, if a society did not possess that individualism, then for that very reason it was not developed enough. Since industrialism produced, or was accompanied by, individualism, something was missing in the Japanese situation as it failed to produce a consequent parallel phenomenon.

Arguably a case can be made to support the view that in the absence of corresponding individualism, certain individual freedoms and rights cannot be effectively realised. The need for evidence in such an argument would shift from individualism to rights and their fulfilment. What cannot be satisfactorily argued, however, is that individualism *qua* individualism, Western style, is good for all societies. In doing that we merely attribute moral property to an historical phenomenon which is confined to a handful of Western countries. Then there are different expressions of individualism, from John Locke to Bertrand Russell in Britain, Thomas Jefferson to John Dewey in the United States, and Voltaire to Camus in France. Which one of these do we then prescribe to a non-Western political society, to enable it to keep up with us in terms of what we think is morally desirable?

The kind of individualism which certain Western countries have historically experienced, and carefully cultivated, no doubt became vital for the sustaining of their own liberal political institutions. Nevertheless, it will be difficult to formulate a universally valid prescription from such experiences for all societies. Moreover, the 'individualistic ethic of the individuated man', as Dore called it,[57] has not always been as morally unassailable, even in Western societies, as is claimed by some of these scholars.

Imposed Democratic Institutions

A 'democratic revolution' was imposed on Japan by the Allied Occupation between 1945 and 1952. During that period a large number of traditional institutions were dismantled and new ones, similar to those in Western countries and, in particular, in the United States, were established.[58] The question is, what happened to those institutions in their actual operations, given the fact that they had to work within an environment where traditions of governance had been very different? To what extent has the operation of new institutions, and their underlying normative structure, changed such an environment? Conversely, how did the social and cultural environment influence and shape the operation of such institutions?

Unlike India and China, which deliberately chose their own political institutions, the situation of Japan was similar to some of the countries of Eastern Europe where political institutions were imposed by a conquering power. The Occupation decision-makers first of all dismantled the traditional bases of Japanese social organisation, i.e. 'the divinity and the infallibility' of the Emperor, the preeminent position of the ruling oligarchy and the army, land tenure, public rituals and the educational system. For the first time in her history, Japan officially handed over decision-making powers to 'the sovereign people' and their elected deputies.[59] In other words, what the Occupation authority did was to superimpose certain liberal legal and political institutions, of a Western variety, on a society which was deeply rooted in the norms of hierarchy, unquestioned loyalty to the group and superiors, and, above all, group-fused individuals. These norms were bound to interact with those of equality, participation, rule of law, individual rights and electorally-mandated political authority as implicit in liberal legal and political institutions, and affect the existing network of social and political relationships.

Unfortunately, very few studies are available which permit us to glimpse the changing nature of political relationships and the attitude to political authority in general in Japan. What we have, so far, by way of studies of the politics of Japan, relates to political institutions, elections, bureaucracy, state support for a variety of commercial and industrial undertakings, etc. What we do not have, however, are a series of continuing studies which identify and explain the intricacies and actualities of social and political change in Japan. Since the indigenous in Japan exists side by side with what has been borrowed, there are the processes of interaction, interpenetration, and the emergence of the new and different in certain areas of her social and political life.[60] It is precisely those areas which need to be identified and explained by means of refined and reformulated theories of social and political development.

The democratic revolution imposed by the Occupation authority expected Japanese political society to change itself radically, giving up deeply assimilated traditional norms. In Japan's multilayered political society, however, there have been historical deposits of other norms as well. Earlier, Confucianism in Japan had emphasised the virtues of loyalty, filial piety, righteousness, obedience and benevolence. After that the emphasis of *samurais* fell on the virtues of austerity, courage and self-sacrifice. And finally, after the Meiji restoration, *koketai* (national polity) was emphasised as a divine creation requiring unquestioned obedience.[61] In what significant ways do these norms continue to influence the operations of new institutions and the quality of public life in general?

Scholars who have studied the political culture of Japan are deeply impressed by her enormous voter participation. But the question such a phenomenon raises is whether the voters vote to influence major decisions or merely vote out of sense of 'duty to vote', reinforced by traditional norms?[62] In the absence of intensive and continuing studies of public participation, we are unable to get a clearer picture of the nature of political change which has occurred in Japan in recent years.

As we identify more and more peculiarities of the Japanese political process – given the multilayered character of her political society, the interaction between her traditional norms and the norms of new political institutions, affecting the network of social and political relationships and the attitude to political authority in general – the greater will be the need to formulate adequate conceptual tools in order to understand such peculiarities in their own context, rather than as replicates of experiences elsewhere.

Our brief analysis of the three multilayered political societies has been an exercise in reminding ourselves of the need to examine each of them in their historical and cultural contexts, and in emphasising the need for the refinement and reformulation of our conceptual tools in understanding them. In that sense it has been an exercise in stocktaking the shortcomings of our intellectual approaches and the inadequacies of our conceptual tools. The corpus of theoretical knowledge, which is based in the historical experiences of a few countries, and which we have used all these years to understand political development all over the world, is clearly over-stretched and out of its depth when it seeks to explain some of the complex political societies of the non-Western world. Such a corpus, we now realise, not only shows insensitivity to certain crucial aspects of such societies, but it also distorts them. One of the major reasons for this is its underlying assumption that non-Western societies *can* be studied as parallels, or potential parallels, of Western political societies. In this chapter we have sought to emphasise the view that such an approach is misconceived and that, given the historical and cultural background of those societies, such parallels might be limited. We should, therefore, pay greater attention to their actualities and devise adequate conceptual tools to do justice to the understanding of them.

4   Relativism and Universalism in Political Development

In the preceding pages we have argued that some of the assumptions of the corpus of theoretical knowledge that are routinely used in order to examine the complexities of political development have, by and large, distorted our understanding of them. Such assumptions have given rise to certain perspectives which have tended to view the processes of political development as either replicating or deviating from Western political experiences or, indeed, holding on, obdurately, to traditional positions of their own. What such assumptions, and the perspectives generated by them, overlooked, as we also pointed out earlier, were the certain basic 'givens' of situations in the non-Western world. These 'givens' brought to our attention the presence of the diversity of historical and cultural conditions in the non-Western world within which certain borrowed legal and political institutions had to operate. They also indicated the need to identify the different degrees of assimilation, coexistence and conflict between the values and behaviour patterns of traditional societies and those prescribed by borrowed institutions.

In our examination of the political societies of developing countries, it was also argued, we are often inclined to go in search of the parallels with our experiences and situations rather than to examine the actuals in the unfamiliar situations in political societies of developing countries. Such a constraint or distortion is forced on us by our theoretical knowledge, which is based almost entirely on the historical experiences of a few Western countries, and which tends to exclude whatever lies outside it.

Any examination of the historical and cultural contexts of a political society inevitably pushes us in the direction of relativism. Nevertheless, we shall argue in this chapter that while certain aspects of the non-Western world ought to be examined in relativistic terms, taking into account the influence of certain contextual factors, our evaluation and judgement on the basic aspects of their public life, their context-dependence notwithstanding, will have to be based on universalistic norms and standards. Such judgements become necessary in situations where the basic moral imperatives concerning civilised political life, affecting *all* human societies, are involved. Such a position requires a set of arguments which can justify relativistic as well as universalistic judgements in different areas of human political development. The presence of such a dual set of standards, which can make allowance for two different situations, might appear logically and philosophically less consistent. Nevertheless, such a position will be necessary if we are to address ourselves to the actualities of the world of political development rather than merely satisfy the logical standard of consistency.

Such a dualistic position, of relativistic as well as universalistic standards, goes directly against our heritage of Greek and Kantian rationalism, where norms of judgement have to be universally valid or they become controversial and useless. Historically speaking, we find ourselves in a curious position. We already have norms of judgement which we formulated much in advance of a sufficient understanding of the non-Western world. And as we come to know more about such a world, we are increasingly forced to make two choices. First, to ignore the distinctiveness of the social and political experience of the non-Western world and thereby continue to apply those norms which have been developed and refined since the days of classical Greece. Second, to restrict the validity of such norms to certain basic moral imperatives relating to the quality of public life, universally speaking, and then to supplement those norms by means of relativistic ones in order to judge situations which are context-dependent and context-shaped. This will no doubt plunge us into a controversy as to where we draw the line. Such a controversy is pretty widespread in other social science disciplines – particularly in anthropology. Since students of political development have so far steered clear of this controversy, they have also missed out on the need to do some fresh thinking on the problem.

Finally, the chapter will also examine the inadequacy of a cognitive approach whereby we expect the non-Western world to be like us, after they have attained their evolutionary political maturity. If not following in our footsteps, we expect them to have at least a corresponding or a parallel course of development. When they do not, we are inclined to characterise them as deviant. In adopting such approaches, we do not study them as actuals, or as distinctively shaped by their own historical and cultural contexts, but as potential replicates of ourselves.

The chapter is divided into the following parts: (i) unrefined theory and consequent distortions; (ii) postulates, parallels and actuals of political development; (iii) the rationality–relativism controversy and its significance for political development; and (iv) the diversity and essential unity of political development. We shall now examine each of these in some detail.

I   UNREFINED THEORY AND CONSEQUENT DISTORTIONS

The manner in which the corpus of theoretical knowledge in the sub-discipline of political development has grown, especially since the Second World War, has not been very helpful in cultivating sensitivity to the various social and cultural contexts which have influenced the phenomenon of development differently in different parts of the world. It has, on the contrary, encouraged indifference towards context-dependent aspects of the operations of various transplanted institutions and the quality of public life which they provided. Also implicit in such an indifference is the unwillingness to identify or formulate new and universally valid notions of what is morally and politically important to public life the world over, despite the fact of their context-influenced diversities. What was done instead was to project political values, implicit in Western historical experiences, *as* universal values. Failure to refine a variety of speculative theories used – in the face of challenges from more rigorous, specific, micro, historical, empirical, anthropological and longitudinal researches – resulted in the inability to recognise diversity of political development, on the one hand, and a persistent exploration into what ought to constitute a universally valid core of moral and public concerns, on the other. Unrefined theories of development therefore not only overlooked the fact of political diversity but also an identifiable unity of core concerns within it.

In the 1950s and 1960s, students of political development welcomed the behavioural theorists and their approach to research which had itself drawn heavily from the conceptual resources of Max Weber, Talcott Parsons and other social theorists. They were welcomed because of their ability to pull the study of politics out of the 'rut' of institutional formalism and provide it with a new approach to studying individual and group behaviour in politics.[1]

Within the study of political development, however, the new behavioural approach itself became a victim of yet another 'rut'. While lip-service was paid, in such studies, to the importance of social and cultural contexts within which political behaviour was examined, the corpus of theoretical knowledge used, to formulate questions, analyse data and present them in conceptualised form, did not always show sensitivity to such contexts. Moreover, the theories and concepts used were rarely pretested or refined after a spell of field research. For all practical purposes, therefore, such theories and concepts, unpretested and unrefined, remained in charge of research from start to finish.

It was in this connection that Gunnar Myrdal, in his monumental work, *Asian Drama*, expressed his criticism of the data collected on developing countries, with the help of such theories and concepts, as having little or no relevance to the social reality of those regions.[2]

In the conduct of actual research, as we all know, unless we emphasise the testing aspect of our theoretical formulations, we end up by 'validating' them. That is to say we are, more often than not, inclined to pay more attention to facts which support them than run counter to them.

Initially one does need theoretical direction, no matter how very speculative, tentative or exploratory. But once in the field, one has to be an open-minded, open-eyed researcher and try to scrutinise, as best as one can, the limits and validity of assertions implicit in one's theories. It was for this reason that Karl Popper prescribed 'the ethic of falsifiability', as Earnest Gellner put it, to all researchers. Popper wanted them to go in search of precisely those evidences which ran counter to their theoretical assertions. And to facilitate such a procedure he even wanted statements to be so formulated that they could easily be tested, confirmed or falsified. For him, the falsifiability of a statement therefore became one of its scientific attributes. He had no illusion as to the strength of human intellectual passion wanting to prove that everything they are attached to is right and true.[3]

One's theory at best supplies one with a cognitive map to one's research terrain. After such an initial function, its usefulness to the researcher may or may not survive. Once in the terrain, one has to build new conceptual directions on the spot, to be able to go into alleys and byways never even thought of while formulating the initial theory. And when the first round of field research comes to an end, one tends to grow out of one's initial theoretical direction because it is only a speculative exercise in reaching out to the reality.

The new conceptual formulations, to interpret new revelations in field research, and often formulated on the spot and for specific problems, have to be pieced together. In such a process of piecing together one may retain whatever survives the test of scrutiny, in the form of bits and pieces of one's initial speculative theory. These together, or in part, may or may not survive the second round of field research, giving rise to yet another attempt at theoretical formulations. Each instalment of our enhanced understanding of social reality takes a toll of part of those speculative theoretical formulations attempted in advance of such an understanding.

Such a process can go on almost indefinitely. Those of us who were involved in longitudinal research exercises can recall the number of wreckages, or partial wreckages, of previously held, some of them very dearly, theoretical positions.

Finally, the last of one's theoretical reconstructions takes place when one is writing out one's findings. Consequently, to attribute imperishability to theoretical constructions, prior to field research or indeed at any time, and to let the same theory direct research from one end to the other, is not fully to understand the sequences, and the interrelated functions of theory and field research, in one's cognitive process. The successive stages of our understanding of social reality are in fact built on the successive wreckages of theory. The more rigorous and intensive our research, the greater the number of attempts at refinement and reformulation of theory.

In the study of political development of the non-Western world, the uses of theory and behavioural research, instead of helping us to grasp its actualities, have been in the direction of telling us where it runs parallel to the Western experience and where it has been following a deviant course from it. Even before grasping the peculiarities of the non-Western world, the interpretations of it are couched in terms of either sameness with a difference, and therefore parallel, or unapprovingly different, and therefore deviant.

II   POSTULATES, PARALLELS AND ACTUALS

The routine emphasis on studying parallels instead of, and at the expense of, actuals, and on judging political societies and their development experiences in terms of sameness, or sameness with a difference, or indeed deviance from an assumed absolute norm, has prevented scholars from paying attention to the context-influenced pluralities of such societies. Equally misleading has been the excessive, and sometimes exclusive, emphasis on model-building whereby, for the sake of argument, the social reality and its characteristics are initially reduced to a set of postulates and then, with the help of deductions from such postulates, attempts are made to establish a correspondence between such characteristics and social reality. Under the circumstances, deductions from such postulates are endowed with certain 'contents' which are supposed to square with reality. In academia, especially, so very widespread is the exercise of assuming correspondence between deductions from one's postulates and social reality that scholars do not even bother to question their equations.

In this section we shall once again underline the uniqueness of the political experiences of some of the developing countries and then discuss some of the characteristics of approaches to understanding them in terms of postulates, parallels and actuals.

The encounter of non-Western political societies with the countries of Western Europe, particularly after the late eighteenth century, was, as the distinguished Indian historian Panikkar has pointed out, of a special kind. In the earlier period European traders, pirates and soldiers came in contact with the indigenous population in different regions of the world through commerce, plunder and war. However, after the eighteenth century, countries such as Britain and France were themselves undergoing rapid social change. Such changes were reflected in their own political ideals, new public institutions and philosophies of government. The encounter of such societies with the relatively fragmented societies of the non-Western world – with their pre-industrial economies, near-stagnant social organisations and highly personalised forms of political authority – was bound to leave behind a lasting influence. There was now much to learn, emulate and borrow from these two great European powers.

By the late eighteenth century, Britain and France had established a secure base for the industrialisation of their economy, established political institutions which had not only accommodated entrepreneurial activity but had also widened the base of political participation, transformed the notion of political authority in social contractual terms, deeply involved themselves in explorations towards a greater measure of social equality, reformed their archaic legal system, developed non-political bureaucracy, and above all broadened the base of education to serve and stimulate interest in the development of a wide range of social, economic and scientific activities. The end of the eighteenth century, therefore, witnessed in Britain and France the fruitful convergence of a wide range of activity together with a basic social change which transformed the quality of public life in them. It was an encounter with such countries which deeply shook the indigenous institutions and the social fabric of the non-Western political societies. As the encounter penetrated deeper, during the colonial rule, some of those institutions started disintegrating or were allowed to remain in form only. Examples of these were to be found in the princely states of India and the tribal chiefdoms of Africa. New administrative, revenue, judicial and military systems were transplanted from colonial centres and were suitably modified over a period to protect colonial interests. Modified versions of such institutions, as a result of the pressure of nationalist agitation, survived long after colonial rule had ended.

Furthermore, the growth of a new international system – laws and conventions governing trade and commerce, diplomatic activity, war and peace, foreign aid, technological assistance, etc. – created yet another level of institution-building with outward similarities between Western and non-Western political societies.

Finally, there was the exposure of the elite to Western education, political ideals and public institutions. That too resulted in the emulation of some of the public institutions and practices, especially when such an elite came to power.

But while such changes were introduced at the institutional level, the contexts within which they had to operate were different in different societies. Such contexts vitally influenced and shaped the character and effectiveness of such institutions. The operations of such institutions were also shaped by the traditional attitudes to authority, the social and cultural norms, and also the patterns of political relationships, involving the traditional political distance between the ruler and the ruled, the commitment to new political ideals, political skills, involvement in political process, and, above all, the ability to learn and to improve the effectiveness of one's political involvement.

In each of the developing countries, the experience of operating new political institutions has been different. This is because the context within which they have to function, and the consequent public life which they provide, is different. They therefore call for the study of the *actuals* of the operation of political institutions, and of the character of public life, with reference to the historical and cultural contexts of each of them. To study them either as *parallels* or as deviants from a postulated model of Western experience does not do justice to them. Let us examine this in some detail.

Postulates

In all cognitive processes, one has initially to formulate the problem for research, and the strategy needed to examine it, within the framework of one's own postulational system. By means of such an approach, one postulates in advance of either detailed analysis or empirical investigation what one's problem of enquiry consists of and how far it can be broken down into its analytic components so as to make it manageable for the data-gathering, analysis, testing, presentation, etc. to follow.

Similarly, what one does as a researcher of political societies of the non-Western world is to 'bring' within one's set of postulates, or postulational system, the components which one thinks are significant to the understanding of the specific aspects of the problems in which one is interested.

To such a set of postulates, one also attributes postulate-content. That helps one, in preliminary discussion and analysis, to treat postulate-contents as real or as data. Then there is the likelihood of a self-deceiving error. This occurs when one takes for granted the correspondence between postulate-content, which one has attributed, and the political reality that one wants to study.

A large portion of our *initial* thinking and preparation for research takes place at such a postulational level. Depending upon which social research approach we subscribe to, we then make a decision whether to go beyond the postulational approach for our further, and more realistic, understanding of social and political phenomena.

But even when we do, not all postulates of our inquiry can be fully checked out, refined, or replaced by more plausible ones. What can be done, and is done by careful students of social and political research, is to start questioning and examining the validity of the assumed correspondence of postulates to social reality by devising research strategies to look into historical material and/or conduct empirical investigation to assure oneself of the accuracy of such a correspondence.

Such a step becomes necessary for two specific reasons. First, our theoretical speculation, especially in development studies, takes place with the help of postulates which are grounded in a prior understanding of the Western development process. Consequently, we cannot jump from our understanding of such a process in the West to other parts of the world with the help of our postulates. Second, while the non-Western world happens to be just one 'world', in actual practice it is a residual term for whatever is not Western. What is often forgotten is that there are enormous differences among countries of the non-Western world and an awesome diversity within most of them. Moreover, as the pace of social change in them is different, the various aspects of their existing complex social reality are further compounded.

Consequently, to begin and end our intellectual inquiry at the level of our postulational exercise is merely to take an initial step *towards* understanding rather than getting down to understanding the actualities of any society. The model-building activity within academia, which often fails to go beyond its initial intellectual explorations, is of this nature. It often does not go beyond the first intellectually exciting stage of speculation with the help of postulates. Such knowledge is not valid beyond the limits of the postulational system on which it rests. It constitutes the initial step of intellectual exploration. By itself it does not constitute an adequate understanding of reality, least of all a necessary and sufficient basis for public policy.

There are scholars who argue in defence of explanations deduced from postulational systems, often implying that their position is similar to logical reasoning and its place in every branch of knowledge and, in particular, in mathematics. In certain branches of knowledge, abstract reasoning is considered to be not only a higher form of reasoning, but also a diviner and identifier of logical structures within reality, and of relationships between two or more sets of facts, which are not discernible to our senses. Then there are others who argue that abstract knowledge precedes and follows empirical knowledge in establishing a relationship between facts. Such a controversy has continued from Socrates through to Kant and Wittgenstein.

The postulational system approach used by political development theorists, however, never reached such a degree of sophistication. It did not even reach the level of sophistication of mathematical economists. In the case of the former, it was often an easy way out of the obligation of collecting hard-nosed data to make good their theoretical claims, something which the anthropologists, who also do most of their research in non-Western societies, have done unfailingly since Malinowski.

Parallels

Our first impulse in using the corpus of theoretical knowledge, which is entirely grounded in Western social and political experience, to understand the non-Western world, is to find out how much the latter can be identified, analysed, interpreted and explained in terms of the former. In such an approach what we often do, therefore, is to go in search of the parallels with Western political experience in the non-Western world. And when we go in search of parallels, what we do in fact is to identify either the sameness with, or the differences within such sameness from, Western experiences. Accordingly, our understanding of the sameness, or the differences within sameness (deviance), *is* with reference to Western experiences. In a sense such an approach is inescapable if we conduct our inquiry strictly with the help of our existing corpus of theoretical knowledge. At the moment, that is the only body of ideas we have. Moreover, it is difficult for us to start with the assumption that if we merely confine ourselves to what such a body of ideas has provided, we shall end up by distorting our understanding of what we want to know. Consequently, what we end up with in our search for parallels – parallels with a world that is familiar to us in a world that is relatively less familiar – is what we can infer, in terms of similarities and differences, from what we ourselves are.

Such an approach of seeking out parallels operates at three different levels: identification, analysis and reportage.

With the help of the background of our problems, we want to identify similar problems and even a similar background to them in developing countries. Similarly, if we can see a causal or correlational relationship between such a background and the phenomenon that it gave rise to in the Western world, then we go in search of a replication of such a relationship in developing countries as well. Such an approach makes us less and less sensitive to the presence of other factors giving rise to different problems in the non-Western background.

The same may be true of analysis. We might attribute analytic similarity or analytic difference between specific problems or situations under investigation in Western and/or non-Western worlds which may or may not be the case in existential fact.

Finally, the way we pursue our reportage of findings is very much influenced by the dominant theoretical controversy in the mainstream of social and political theory. If the current style of theoretical dis-

cussion leans heavily on the concepts of class, structural–
functionalism, centre–periphery, dependency theory, etc., we tend
to couch our findings and their reportage within a parallel conceptual framework. None of these concepts, nor the controversies surrounding them, may be wholly or partly relevant to the problems
of developing countries which we may happen to examine.

Actuals

In recent years some progress has been made in the study of political development by means of examination of the various social and
cultural contexts which exercise influence on the operations of political institutions and public life in general. Increasingly, greater attention is being paid to historical antecedents, anthropological studies
and, above all, to the rapidly maturing indigenous scholarship with
its deep understanding of the complexity of social and political life.

Despite such gains, the study of the actualities of political development, with reference to historical and cultural contexts, is often
vitiated by the scholarly fascination with dominant theoretical
approaches. Such approaches are invariably rooted in Western
experiences and to that extent they introduce an element of distortion in the study of the actuals of political development in any non-
Western region. In Chapters 2 and 3, we referred to innumerable
instances of the need to study the actuals of political development
with the help of refined and reformulated theoretical approaches.

The study of the actuals, in their own contextual background, has
stimulated and sustained a lively debate over the problem of relativism and universalism, particularly among anthropologists, for more
than a century. A polarity in their positions on this particular problem has not in any way diminished their interest in the study of the
influence exerted by cultural forces on social institutions. Such a controversy has not been fully appreciated, so far, by students of political development. Moreover, in the case of students of political
development, there is the additional problem of evaluation and judgement on the quality of public life which they study. A number of them
try to play it safe, equivocate or mask their evaluations in excruciating
jargon so as to qualify for another round of research grants and per-
mission from the host country where they are doing their research.
Such a scholarly limitation has also been one of the major factors
in the neglect of the actuals of public life in developing countries.

III THE RATIONALITY–RELATIVISM CONTROVERSY

In Chapter 1 we examined the problem of Western bias in the study of non-Western societies and the manner in which the controversy surrounding universalism and relativism has sought to sensitise us to its presence. In this section we shall once again return to that controversy with a view to grasping its significance for the problem of evaluation and judgement on the quality of social and political life. In certain branches of knowledge, so great has been the concern over this controversy on the part of some scholars that they believe that human knowledge will not be able to make much progress unless some of the central issues raised by it are satisfactorily resolved. At the one extreme we have thinkers like Earnest Gellner who believe that unless we exorcise the spectre of relativism, which has begun to haunt various branches of human knowledge, there will be 'a cognitive anarchy'.[4] At the other extreme, we have relativists like Barry Barnes and David Bloor who hold the view that 'there are no context-free or super-cultural norms of rationality'.[5]

The controversy centres around intellectual as well as moral issues. Such issues concern the source of standards of truth, canons of reasoning and norms of individual and public good. Some scholars argue that these are context-dependent, whereas others claim their universal validity. The proponents of dependence of truth, reasoning and good – on social and cultural contexts – have argued that to consider these as context-independent is merely arbitrarily to universalise the validity of predominant Western views on the subject. Their critics, on the other hand, have contended that, notwithstanding such arbitrarily generalised notions, what is ultimately true, logical or good will have a reasoning of its own rather than the cultural support of this or that group.

Let us now take a few examples of the arguments of certain major participants in the controversy. Karl Mannheim, in his *Ideology and Utopia*, argued that: 'there are modes of thought which cannot be adequately understood as long as their social origins are obscured'. Further, 'it is not men in general who think, or even the isolated individuals who do the thinking, but men in certain groups . . . '[6] So from the author's point of view, in the shaping of human thought, its social origin as well as group perspectives have played an important part.

Mannheim, however, hesitated from taking an extreme relativistic position, of making notions of truth entirely relative to their social contexts. He did not want students of society and philosophy to ignore the fact that while truth and falsity depended on logical criteria – which were independent of social contexts – what was believed to be true and good, and human actions based on such beliefs, had their own social and group contexts and origins. Mannheim thus remained ambivalent.

Such ambivalence was also noticeable in the ideas of Lévy-Bruhl. He noticed an altogether different mode of thought and action in 'primitive' tribes from the one that people in the West were used to. According to him, the primitives 'live, think, feel, move, and act in a world which at a number of points does not coincide with ours'.[7]

Consequently, he believed that we in the West may have to make allowances for what the 'primitives' think of as true and good. However, like Mannheim, he too hesitated in taking the extreme step in the direction of relativism by maintaining that there cannot be compartmentalised 'primitive' truth and 'civilised' truth.

A much more extreme position on relativism was taken by Winch, Whorf and Kuhn in their respective fields. Winch had argued that language plays an enormous part in determining what belongs to the realm of reality. Moreover, 'criteria of logic . . . arise out of, and are only intelligible in the context of, ways of living or modes of social life'.[8] In other words, to Winch, language, together with the network of social relationships, deeply influence not only human thought but even the canons of reasoning themselves.

A similar emphasis, especially on the part played by language in logical analysis, was put by Whorf. In his words:

> when anyone, as a natural logician, is talking about reason, logic, and the laws of correct thinking, he is apt to be simply marching in step with purely grammatical facts that have somewhat of a background character in his own language or family of languages but are by no means universal in all languages and in no sense a common substratum of reason.[9]

The greatest support for epistemological relativism, however, came at the hands of the well-known historian of science, Thomas Kuhn. He argued that paradigms, which in themselves are not context-free, deeply influence the perception, reasoning and activity of scientists in general: 'The historian of science may be tempted to exclaim that when paradigms change, the world itself changes with them.'[10] Moreover, in a situation where a scientist is faced with the problem of having to make 'a paradigm choice', it is not his abstract reasoning that ultimately determines which of the choices is logical or true, but what the community of scientists at any given time thinks is right. In his words: 'there is no standard higher than the assent of the community'.[11]

In the sociology of knowledge, Barry Barnes and David Bloor have argued in recent years that scientific knowledge requires a relativistic approach, because disciplines such as anthropology, sociology, the history of institutions and cognitive psychology, which account for 'the diversity of systems of knowledge',[12] require a diverse and relativistic approach to the understanding of human and social problems.

From the point of view of the relativists, the rationalists, in their claim to a context-free approach to knowledge, merely tend to view their own position as morally superior. From such a position they often pass what they claim to be universally valid judgements. To relativists, such a claim is indefensible, for those who examine are as much context-dependent as those who are examined. Consequently, no one should be solely in charge of passing judgements on the assumed claims to rationality, objectivity and context-independence.[13] And as long as a relativist can live with a situation where there is no ultimate truth as certified by a rationalist, he does not miss out on anything. Moreover, such a position also shifts the discussion from the ultimate truth, arrived at with the help of abstract reasoning, to more realistic questions of how a variety of beliefs came to be held as true beliefs by certain groups.

The rationality–relativism controversy is of great significance to the study of political development. It is a controversy which has affected so many branches of human knowledge. In anthropology, in particular, where, as in political development, scholars go out and study other societies, there has been a growing awareness of possible ethnocentric biases involved in such studies and, above all, of the inadequacies of conceptual tools, of canons of reasoning and of the comparative standards used for evaluating different cultures. By contrast, students of political development have yet to show any awareness of the problems to which their own perceptions, tools of analysis and judgement give rise.

Then there is an additional problem in the case of students of political development. Unlike anthropologists, they need to make an evaluation and judgement on the quality of public life in any political society they study. It is in such a field, which is of basic concern to political development, that the rationality–relativism controversy raises some of the most difficult questions.

While such a controversy has created a polarisation of cognitive approaches, as we saw in the earlier part of this section, the subdiscipline of political development cannot remain confined to such epistemological questions only. It has to move on to yet another function of evaluating and judging the quality of public life in every society. For in the very notion of political development, ideals of public life and the standards of evaluation of attaining them are implicit. So as a subdiscipline it needs, like anthropology, a sensitivity to the context-dependent nature of political institutions and their operations, on the one hand, and a universally valid notion of what should constitute what I have later called a 'public minimum',[14] on the other. The former calls for a relativistic approach and the latter for a universalistic approach. There again the question is whether what we regard as a universally desirable 'minimum' of public life should be entirely based on Western experience of it or should it also try to go beyond it? What we need, therefore, is a reformulated notion of a universally valid standard, or at least an exploration towards it, which can help us evaluate and judge matters of basic human, moral and public concern.

Any intellectual position which emphasises two sets of standards of judgement can be criticised for duality and even inconsistency. One of the legitimate questions which a dualistic position must face, however, is when does the domain of universalistic judgements concede ground to relativistic judgements? Would not the domain of relativistic judgements become an area of escape, rationalisation and indulgence?

Such a position of dualism, therefore, is bound to become untidy, logically untenable and intellectually messy. Nevertheless, it will reflect a compromise which is very much in evidence in the existential world. There are certain practices of social groups amongst us which we accept as peculiar to them, and, as long as their consequences do not spill over into the wider public domain, we tend to tolerate them.

Moreover, in political development in particular, where evaluation of public policy and public behaviour becomes as important as the cognitive efforts to understand them, we cannot merely settle for a polarity of intellectual positions of relativism and universalism. We have to go beyond it.

One of the areas of examination of political development in any society is the level of understanding which people show towards various segments of society so that they can live in an atmosphere of give and take and mutual accommodation without violating the universally shared moral and public concerns.

In taking into account our own positions on dualism and compromise, we cannot ignore the fact of our intellectual heritage of Greek rationalism which jealously leans towards universalism. Unless we presuppose the universality of 'laws of logic' and the 'criterion of truth' in making comparative and evaluative judgements, we might give rise to intellectually chaotic conditions.[15] Moreover, to be able to *judge* a variety of relativistic positions, we need universally valid canons of logic and the criteria of determining truth.[16]

Such intellectual problems notwithstanding, the study of political development can ignore neither the need for relativism in understanding context-dependent aspects of institutions and political behaviour of people, nor the need for universalism for evaluating and judging those areas of public concerns which affect everyone.

IV   DIVERSITY AND ESSENTIAL UNITY OF POLITICAL DEVELOPMENT

In previous pages we argued that the theoretical knowledge used in the study of political development has not been able to pay sufficient attention, for one reason or another, to the various historical and cultural forces which have influenced the operations of public institutions, indigenous or transplanted, and the quality of public life in general in developing countries. In this section we shall argue that our recognition of their diversity should be treated as the basis for an exploration and formulation of standards which can help us to evaluate and judge the quality of their public life. Such standards, based on an increased sensitivity to context-dependent aspects as well as to moral and public concerns in human governance, universally speaking, are not easy to formulate. Implicit in them, as stated earlier, are the problems of jurisdiction, rationalisation and the possible weakening of moral imperatives when placed side by side with the escapist component of relativism.

A search for what ought to matter most *within* political development, just about anywhere, regardless of the history and culture of any political society, resulted in a few useful attempts which, unfortunately, were not followed up by means of extended works or discussions. The writings of Pye, Riggs, Huntington and Coleman are of note in this respect.

Lucian Pye, after examining a variety of definitions of political development formulated in terms of prerequisites such as an industrialised economy, a modern outlook, widening suffrage, the neutrality of administration, orderly change, etc., came to the conclusion that what is central to political development is an ever-increasing realisation of the ideals of equality, participation and differentiation.[17] The term 'differentiation' came from the structural–functionalists who used it to refer to the specialised institutional capacity of a political system to meet the challenge of new forces in order to maintain itself. The significance of these three political ideals was drawn almost entirely from the central role they have played in the political development of the countries of Western Europe and North America. The significance of such ideals to non-Western societies, which is indeed enormous, was taken for granted. Absent in such an emphasis is a discussion of 'when', 'how' and in 'conjunction' with which other forces these political ideals would become significant in the political development of non-Western societies. Their universal and timeless validity, across historical and cultural divides, was also taken for granted.

A more detailed exposition of the same ideals was provided by Fred Riggs.[18] He argued that the realisation of these ideals would also require what he called 'the new political technology' or, in simpler language, new political skills to be able to work out accommodations for a share in the political power. Without the growth of such skills on the part of the political elite, the political organisation of society will experience a chain of political gyrations and instabilities caused by excessive demands and an equally excessive resistance to them.

Next in this line of argument is the contribution of James Coleman. He argued that equality, capacity and differentiation are the three integral aspects of the 'development syndrome'.[19] They make development, including political development, possible. Emphasis on equality, he believed, would shift social recognition from ascription to achievement; on capacity would underline the importance of systemic capability; and on differentiation of institutions ('contrapuntal interplay'; Smelser) through specialisation would give rise to a new kind of solidarity and integration. Once again, as in the case of Pye, the importance of these values to the non-Western world was taken for granted.

Samuel Huntington and his associate, Joan Nelson, in their *No Easy Choice: Political Participation in Developing Countries*,[20] pointed out that while the universal importance of a number of political values which first crystallised in the West cannot be doubted, the manner in which they affect the course of actual political development elsewhere remains indeterminate. For this purpose, the authors underlined the importance of three goals: economic development; social and economic equality; and political participation. Any emphasis on the precedence of one over the other, they pointed out, would generate certain consequences and imbalances which might be difficult to reverse. Consequently, these values need to be emphasised in their delicate proportion and sequence, which is bound to be different in different political societies, to be able to serve the cause of political development effectively. For the authors, therefore, the choice of emphasis, and the precedence of one over the other, is not easy. Their work shows a rare insight into the actualities of the problems of developing countries.

The political ideals of equality and participation, despite their deep roots in Western experiences, in particular, American and French, are of tremendous significance to developing countries with their deeply institutionalised traditional social hierarchies, and unshrinking political distance between the rulers and the ruled. While, in the countries of the West, the ideals of equality and participation were an outgrowth of prior entrepreneurial economic activity, wanting to reshape legal and political institutions in order to make them permissive of such an activity, their popularisation and embodiment in the constitutions of developing countries was the work of a nationalist political elite which had fought many a battle, in the name of those ideals, against colonial rule. For the realisation of these ideals, therefore, such a difference, in the manner of their introduction, became most significant. In non-Western societies in particular, despite institutional provisions for them, the actual realisation of those ideals, because of their sudden introduction from the top, remained extremely precarious.

As stated earlier, the nationalist elite in the bulk of new countries had effectively used the ideal of political participation to embarrass their colonial rulers, who had boasted their allegiance to those ideals. It had also used it to mobilise its own people. Moreover, since political participation in most colonies was conceded grudgingly, and in instalments, by colonial rulers, it had occupied a central place in political agitation. While in the initial years it was not safe to talk about the termination of colonial rule, there was much less risk in gradually escalating the demand for public participation.

Unlike public participation, the ideal of equality came to have much greater significance after independence from colonial rule. Most colonial powers had left the traditional social organisations of their colonies untouched. In them there were deeply rooted hierarchies which had persisted for centuries. Then there were feudal elements and the neo-rich who had either retained their economic advantage or had actually flourished during colonial rule. They too, therefore, had become the target of agitation. Moreover, the ideology of socialism, which found numerous champions among the nationalist leaders, also added to the attraction of the ideal of equality.

The task of making institutional provisions for the realisation of the ideal of equality, despite disproportionate advantages arising out of the deeply assimilated hierarchy in the traditional social organisation, fell on the constitutional lawyers of the post-independence period. And they made formal provisions for equality, in legal, political and social terms, in the constitutions which they drafted.

But the ideals of political participation and equality, which were enshrined in the constitutions of the post-colonial period, called for a commensurate political capacity to translate a formal institutional provision into a living social and political reality. Before we go on to that, we ought to grasp at this stage the misplaced emphasis on differentiation, as a political ideal, in the literature on political development.

By any account the term 'differentiation' is a fuzzy one, and instead of becoming a tool of analysis, it has become, because of a lack of clarity, a means of clouding the issues involved. Moreover, it has been used in two unconnected senses: as institutional differentiations, meaning specialised goals pursued by different institutions; and occasionally, as an attribute of human political skill by means of which one finds accommodating solutions in situations of competition and conflict. Only in the second sense, in which it is occasionally used, is the concept useful in understanding the problems of developing countries.

Differentiation in the role of institutions, and above all, in their specialised pursuits, became important at certain stages in political development, but what is more important than that to the individual is his political capacity to be able to get response and effective performance from those whom he puts, or finds, in public office. In other words, the focus of such an ideal should have been at the *human* end, emphasising the relationship between human beings and institutions, rather than between institutions themselves. Institutions, or specialised institutions, can serve specialised functions. But their effective functioning can be measured not with reference to their specialised operations, but primarily in terms of the quality of their response to the people they are supposed to serve. The criterion of evaluation thus needs to be shifted from the quality of their operations, in formal institutional terms, to their responses to the demands and needs of those whom they are supposed to serve.

Specialisation as a facet of differentiation, moreover, is a phenomenon which has greater relevance to societies which have attained some measure of a responsive and responsible relationship between individuals and public institutions. But in societies which have experienced enormous political distance between rulers and ruled, and where that distance has been reinforced, in some cases, in post-colonial situations, the central problem is one of the growth of human political capacity to get responses from those in public institutions rather than be served by impersonal, but non-responsive, specialised institutions. Consequently, central to the notion of gradual enjoyment of either political participation, equality or differentiation, is the notion of political capacity. To that we now turn.

Within the developing countries a curious situation was created in the immediate post-colonial period. The nationalist political elite, and the indigenous body of constitutional lawyers, established liberal legal and political institutions, with their implicit norms, and imposed them on social organisations which had their own traditional norms. Such institutions were created in advance of a widespread demand for them, as in the case of the countries of Western Europe and North America. Moreover, they were also created in advance of the growth of a commensurate political capacity to be able to appreciate them and/or use them and, what is more, defend them at a time of illiberal inroads.

In a manner of speaking, in all societies, developed or developing, constitutional or institutional provisions far exceed, in their actual or potential scope, the historical demands in response to which they were created in the first place. Consequently, there is always much more to their provisions than human beings can either exhaust at any one time or develop commensurate political capacity to be able to use.

The institutional provisions for the enjoyment of certain rights and participatory status, and for overcoming social and political inequalities, thus awaited the growth of the political capacity of the citizenry of developing countries. In situations where such liberal legal and political institutions were overrun by civilian or military dictatorships, even their shortlived establishment, arising directly out of movements against colonial rule, had a lasting effect on the thinking of the political elite. Such an elite had to lie low until a suitable opportunity presented itself for it before it could begin to agitate for the revival of such institutions.

In developing countries there has been a deeply ingrained fear of government, no matter who has been in power. Moreover, the traditional political distance between the rulers and the ruled has often been reinforced, or sought to be reinforced, by leaders who feel uncomfortable with criticism and competition for political power. They therefore derive maximum advantage out of political instabilities and upheavals, both to secure absolute power and to rationalise the need for illiberal regimes. Consequently, an emphasis on participation and equality, with corresponding institutional provisions for their enjoyment, did not by themselves go far enough. These ideals and provisions had to await the growth of human political capacity capable of participating in the shaping of public policy, and in seeking response and accountability from those on the other side of the power divide.[21]

Moreover, we need to understand the peculiar nature of impediments to the growth of political capacity in different societies. Such impediments arise as a result of a political society's historical, cultural, religious or economic background. And to make certain political ideals meaningful, and to bring them within the bounds of realisability, we need to know the nature of impediments to them in different societies.[22]

Within the study of political development, therefore, we shall have to explore the norms which are universally valid; norms which need the support of certain auxiliary conditions to become acceptable and realisable universally; and norms which will remain context-dependent and therefore incapable of universal validity. But over and above these, we should also be able to think in terms of norms which constitute what I have called 'the public minimum' and which are, therefore, quintessential to human political development as such.

A growing body of literature has sought to emphasise, mostly from a Western point of view, what a political society *qua* political society ought to have by way of a 'minimum'[23] in its public life. By means of such a 'minimum', it is claimed, we ought to be able to evaluate and judge the conduct of individuals, groups, officials, institutions and corporations in public life. Such a literature is of great significance to developing countries. Since their emergence, their ability gradually to provide such a 'public minimum' has not been as rigorously scrutinised as should have been the case.

A large number of developing countries do not yet have what we mean by the rule of law. After an initially impressive start, a number of them have become victims of highly personalised civilian or military dictatorships, which in turn have emaciated most of their public institutions. Unless such regimes are replaced by the rule of law, whereby men and institutions derive their power of office from the fundamental law of the land, along with customs and traditions, the basic prerequisite condition for any political development worth the name will be absent.

While scholarly literature on political development has emphasised public participation, what the experience of the last three decades in developing countries suggests is that we need also to emphasise certain basic freedoms which make such participation possible. Regardless of historical forces and the cultural contexts of any political society, what we need to emphasise are freedoms of speech, association, press and of seeking political alternatives, peacefully and constitutionally. Integrally connected with these are the independence of the judiciary and the bureaucracy. In recent years, those developing countries which were able to provide these, were also able to sustain a number of their liberal political institutions.

Then there are the problems of equity and social programmes. Societies where wide inequalities of wealth, status, education and opportunity exist tend to keep their citizens at unequal levels of development in general and political development in particular. Similarly, a society which does not make adequate provision for education, employment, social security and medical aid either limits or distracts its citizens from taking an interest in public issues.

One of the major problems in developing countries, particularly in the field of competitive politics, is that of the zero-sum game or the shabby, cruel and sometimes barbarous treatment meted out to political competitors who lose out in an electoral bid for power. Such political societies have to learn to civilise their political conflict. One of the major achievements of Western political societies, in the harsh field of politics, is to have convinced its citizenry that competing for public office is in the best interest of society, a means whereby everyone is best able to judge who will serve his or her interests well. An electoral conflict itself is a contrived and theatred conflict and exists only for the purposes of electing individuals, with majority support, to public office. Among those developing countries where liberal institutions have struck roots, this was one of the most difficult lessons to learn.

Then there is the widespread curse of men in military uniform usurping public office in developing countries. While such takeovers are ostensibly in the name of efficiency and incorruptibility, after a short while in office, such regimes are no better than those they replace. Under no circumstances, therefore, should a military takeover of a functioning civilian government, however incompetent, be allowed to justify itself.

The phenomenon of the abuse of public authority or political corruption, which is fairly widespread in developing countries, should be denounced in no uncertain terms. While no country has been able completely to eradicate it, the extent of political corruption in more developed countries has been very much limited and controlled by means of effective criticism by citizens, the media, party organisations and the judiciary. The corresponding means of checking political corruption in developing countries are not always very effective. It should occupy a primary position in a list of their urgent problems.

While these considerations – ranging from the rule of law, basic freedoms, electorally mandated political authority, etc., through to the need to eradicate abuse of public authority – appear to us in the West as hardly worth talking about, their realisation in the bulk of new political societies is a distant possibility. Consequently, not only do we have to identify what is missing, in that respect, in those political societies, but we must also designate the need for them as an integral part of the 'public minimum' without which civilised political life, regardless of cultural and historical conditions, becomes impossible. Cultural relativism, for instance, should not become a premise for rationalising political brutality. Nor can it be allowed to justify the absence of elections or an independent judiciary. Consequently, to be able to evaluate the quality of public life with reference to the 'minimum' of public life, we do need universalistic criteria which cannot be explained away by means of relativistic arguments.

Within our examination of the problems involved in studying political development, we have one of the most unenviable tasks of balancing the need for relativism, in order to understand genuine differences in the operation of political institutions and public life which are shaped by a diversity of historical and cultural conditions, on the one hand, and universalism, in order to be able to emphasise the basic moral and public minimum without which civilised political life becomes impossible, on the other.

Such a logically untidy position, of coexistence and the balance of relativism and universalism, appears to be more unacceptable in the realm of intellectual reasoning than in the existential world. This is because the latter is always a mix of consistencies and inconsistencies. As intellectuals and thinking men and women of developing countries gain a balanced perspective on their own heritage and a greater awareness of the significance of some of the political values which have come from the West to their own social organisation, they are less likely to discard the notion of public minimum. Nor would they be worried about the inconsistency of relativism and universalism in certain values. What they would nevertheless like to see incorporated, gradually, in such a minimum is the universal significance of some of their *own* experiences and values.

As we begin to pay more attention to the complexity of different political societies, we also realise that they too have contributions to make to human political development as such. Only recently have developing countries emerged from prolonged periods of social destabilisation and/or colonial subjection. They will therefore need time to contribute the significance of their own experiences to human social and political existence as such. In the meantime we would do well to shed our own superciliousness and to cultivate a sensitivity to their possible contribution in the future. Already there is evidence of their contribution in science, technology, commerce, industrial management and agriculture. Their possible contribution in other fields cannot therefore be far behind.

Just by way of illustration, we can refer here to what can be gleaned already from the experiences of the three multilayered political societies: India, China and Japan. The Indians, under the influence of Mahatma Gandhi and Jayaprakash Narayan, developed some of the richest ideas on the theory and practice of political resistance relevant to our times.[24] They also developed some profound notions of the conditions which can prevent political relationships from becoming exploitative relationships. Similarly, the Chinese in the pre- and post-revolutionary period, created, under the persistent influence of Confucian *li*, human and cultural conditions which seek to minimise the harshness of human governance as such. Finally, the Japanese have been able to demonstrate the enormous psychological sense of security, together with economic and political effectiveness, provided by their traditional emphasis on associated living and acting, subsequently adapted to modern conditions. As opposed to the individualism of Western societies, which is vastly exaggerated and elevated to the level of a moral principle, associated living and working has a deep significance for our social existence as well as for our habits of work.

Inferences derived from all these principles and practices have the potential to become integral parts of the widely-shared notions of 'public minimum'. What we need to do, therefore, is to bring back within the framework of our discussion on problems of political development the experiences of all political societies.

Notes and References

CHAPTER 1

1. See in this connection Paul Streeten's fascinating paper 'The Limits of Development Research', *World Development*, 2, 10–12 (1974) 16.
2. Reinhard Bendix, *Embattled Reason: Essays in the Sociology of Knowledge* (Oxford University Press, 1970) p. viii.
3. Elbaki Hermassi, *The Third World Reassessed* (California University Press, 1980) p. 3. My italics.
4. Quoted by Shlomo Avinere on Hegel in *Hegel's Theory of the Modern State* (Cambridge University Press, 1972) p. 224.
5. 'The British Rule in India' by Karl Marx in *Karl Marx on Colonialism and Modernism*, ed. Shlomo Avineri (New York: Anchor Books, 1969) pp. 88–95.
6. See in this connection 'The Ethnocentrism of the Social Science Implications For Research and Policy' by Howard J. Wiarda, *The Review of Politics*, 43, 2 (April 1981).
7. Bendix, *Embattled Reason*, p. 269.
8. Wiarda, 'The Ethnocentrism of Social Science Implications For Research and Policy', p. 172.
9. Barrington Moore Jr, *Social Origins of Dictatorship and Democracy: Lord and the Peasant in the Making of the Modern World* (Boston, Mass.: Beacon Press, 1960).
10. Talcott Parsons, *The Social System* (New York: Free Press of Glencoe, 1951).
11. W. W. Rostow, *Politics and the Stages of Growth* (Cambridge University Press, 1971).
12. A. K. F. Organski, *The Stages of Political Development* (New York: Alfred A. Knopf, 1965).
13. Daniel Lerner, 'Communication System and Social Systems: A Statistical Exploration in History and Policy', *Behavioral Science*, 2 (1957).

14. Bendix, *Embattled Reason*, p. 271.
15. Also see in this connection Hermassi, *Third World Reassessed*, p. 9.
16. Alex Inkeles and David Smith, *Becoming Modern: Individual Change in Six Developing Countries* (Cambridge, Mass.: Harvard University Press, 1974).
17. See in this connection a swing in the other direction and unqualified praise for the Japanese approach to modernisation and industrial management in Ezra Vogel's *Japan as Number One* (Cambridge, Mass.: Harvard University Press, 1979). In this work Vogel argues that 'Japan, with its great sense of group orientation, more recent emergence from feudalism, and government-led modernization, has developed solutions for many of these (labor–management adversarial relations; internal migrations; and social change in general) problems that America, with its more individualistic and legalistic history, might never have invented. America's transition to industrialisation did not require the central direction nor the high level of government and business cooperation required of a borrower. Now that post industrial America, too, requires higher level of cooperation and more central leadership oriented to modern economic order, there is no reason why America could not borrow and adapt Japanese models which, with different tradition, it could not have originally created' (p. 253).
18. See in this connection Edward Shils, *Between Tradition and Modernity: The Indian Intellectuals* (The Hague: Mouton, 1959).
19. Robert A. Levine and Donald T. Campbell, *Ethnocentricism: Theories of Conflict, Ethnic Attitudes, and Group Behavior* (New York: John Wiley and Sons, 1971) p. 1.
20. Ibid., p. 9.
21. Ibid., p. 137.
22. Daniel Lerner, *The Passing of Traditional Society: Modernising the Middle East* (London: Collier-Macmillan, 1958) p. ix.
23. Ibid., p. 46.
24. Gabriel A. Almond and James Coleman (eds), *The Politics of the Developing Areas* (Princeton University Press, 1960) p. 4.
25. Ibid., p. 17.
26. Ibid., p. 7.
27. Ibid., p. 64.
28. Gabriel A. Almond and Sidney Verba, *The Civic Culture: Political Attitudes and Democracy in Five Nations* (Princeton University Press, 1963) p. 7.

29. Ibid., p. 473.
30. Gabriel A. Almond and Bingam Powell, *Comparative Government: A Developmental Approach* (Boston: Little, Brown, 1966) p. 6.
31. Ibid., p. ix.
32. Gabriel A. Almond, *Political Development: Essays in Heuristic Theory* (Boston: Little, Brown, 1970) p. 21.
33. Lucian W. Pye, *Politics, Personality, and Nation-Building: Burma's Search For Identity* (Yale University Press, 1962) p. xv.
34. Ibid., p. 5.
35. See for the actual details of this process my longitudinal study published under the title of *Democracy and Political Change in Village India: A Case-study* (New Delhi: Orient Longman, 1972).
36. Marvin Harris, *The Rise of Anthropological Theory: A History of Theories of Culture* (New York: Thomas Y. Crowell, 1968) p. 373.
37. Ibid., p. 259.
38. Pye, *Politics, Personality, and Nation-Building*, p. ix.
39. Ibid., pp. xiv–xv.
40. See in this connection E. R. Leach, *Rethinking Anthropology* (London: University of London, The Athlone Press, 1961) p. 4.
41. Karl Popper, *Open Society and Its Enemies* (London: Routledge & Kegan Paul, 1966) vol. II, pp. 213–16.
42. E. E. Evans-Prichard, *Social Anthropology* (London: Cohen & West, 1951) *passim*, p. 22.
43. John Beattie, *Other Cultures: Aims, Methods, and Achievements in Social Anthropology* (London: Cohen & West, 1964) p. 9.
44. Marvin Harris, *The Rise of Anthropological Theory*, p. 250.
45. Bronislaw Malinowski, *Argonauts of Western Pacific* (London: G. Routledge & Sons, 1922) p. 3.
46. Evans-Prichard, *Social Anthropology*, pp. 2–3.
47. Ibid., pp. 54–5.
48. Beattie, *Other Cultures*, p. 67.
49. Gregory Bateson, *Naven* (Cambridge University Press, 1936) p. 278.
50. 'African Traditional Thought and Western Science' by Robin Horton in *Rationality*, ed. Bryan Wilson (Oxford: Basil Blackwell, 1970).

CHAPTER 2

1. Reinhard Bendix, *Nation-Building and Citizenship* (California

University Press, 1964) *passim*, pp. 2–5.
2. Richard P. Appelbaum, *Theories of Social Change* (Chicago: Markham Publishing Co., 1970) *passim*, pp. 21–55.
3. Alex Inkeles and David Smith, *Becoming Modern*.
4. 'Developmental Change and the Nature of Man' by Morris Opler in *Perspectives on Developmental Change*, ed. Art Gallaher Jr (Lexington: University of Kentucky Press, 1968) pp. 20–3.
5. Fred W. Riggs maintained that 'Western civilization itself is an extraordinarily complex mixture of cultural trends, and borrowing nations may be quite selective in choosing what to assimilate'. See in this connection his 'Political Aspects of Developmental Change' in *Perspectives on Developmental Change*, ed. Art Gallaher Jr, p. 144.
6. See in this connection Louis Hartz *et al.*, *The Founding Fathers of New Society: Studies in the History of the United States, Latin America, South Africa, Canada, Australia* (New York: Harcourt, Brace & World, 1964).
7. Robert Nisbet, *Tradition and Revolt: Historical and Sociological Essays* (New York: Random House, 1968) p. 4.
8. Alexis de Tocqueville, *Democracy in America* (New York: Vintage Books, 1945) vol. I, p. 3.
9. *Alexis de Tocqueville: Selected Writings*, ed. John Stone and Stephen Mennell (Chicago University Press, 1980) pp. 170–1.
10. Ibid., p. 166.
11. 'The Social Psychology of World Religions' by Max Weber in *From Max Weber: Essays in Sociology*, ed. H. H. Gerth and C. Wright Mills (Oxford University Press, 1948) p. 268.
12. Ibid., *passim*, pp. 268–9.
13. Max Weber, *The Protestant Ethic and the Spirit of Capitalism* (New York: Charles Scribner and Sons, 1958). With a foreword by R. H. Tawney, p. 2.
14. Ibid., pp. 181–3.
15. Max Weber, *General Economic History* (Glencoe, Illinois: Free Press, 1950) *passim*, pp. 27–111.
16. Ibid., *passim*, pp. 275–313.
17. See in this connection 'Imperial Germany and Industrial Revolution' by Thorstein Veblen in *Thorstein Veblen*, ed. Bernard Rosenberg (New York: Thomas Y. Crowell, 1963).
18. Quoted by Reinhard Bendix, *Nation-Building and Citizenship*, pp. 8–9.
19. Ibid., p. 9.

20. 'Preconditions of Development: A Comparison of Japan and Germany' by Reinhard Bendix in *Aspects of Social Change in Modern Japan*, ed. R. P. Dore (Princeton University Press, 1967) p. 28.
21. See in this connection Elbaki Hermassi, *The Third World Reassessed* (California University Press, 1980) *passim*, pp. 96–9. Also see James A. Bill and Carl Leiden, *Politics in the Middle East* (Toronto: Little, Brown, 1979).
22. *Political Elite in the Middle East*, ed. George Lenczowski (Washington D.C.: American Enterprise Institute for Public Policy Research) p. 11.
23. James A. Bill and Carl Leiden, *Politics in the Middle East*, p. 135.
24. See in this connection Marlene Hancock's 'The Role of the Elite in Political Development: The Case of Saudi Arabia' (unpublished MA thesis: Simon Fraser University, 1982).
25. See in this connection 'Opposition and Control in Turkey' by Serif Mardin, *Government and Opposition*, vol. 3 (1966).
26. See for details of the complex processes of learning the dos and don'ts of operating liberal political institutions in various countries, A. H. Somjee, *Political Society in Developing Countries* (London: Macmillan, 1984).
27. Claudio Veliz, *The Centralist Tradition of Latin America* (Princeton University Press, 1980) p. 3.
28. Latin American scholars have produced a rich literature on 'corporatism'. Their interpretations and explanations of it have a fairly wide range. Anderson, for instance, regards corporatism as a broad pattern which indicates the essential features of the politics of Latin American countries; Wiarda identifies ideological strands within it; Collier, Erikson, Glade, Kaufman, Malloy, Purcell, Stevens and Weinstein view it as a flexible rather than rigid political order; and Schmitter and O'Donnell view it as an authoritarian–bureaucratic phenomenon. See in this connection Howard J. Wiarda, *Corporatism and National Development in Latin America* (Boulder, Colorado: West View Press, 1981).
29. Ibid., pp. 215–16.
30. 'Corporatism and the Question of the State' by Guillermo O'Donnell in *Authoritarianism and Corporatism in Latin America*, ed. James M. Malloy (University of Pittsburg Press, 1977).

CHAPTER 3

1. 'Preconditions of Development: A Comparison of Japan and Germany' by Reinhard Bendix in *Aspects of Social Change in Modern Japan*, ed. R. P. Dore (Princeton University Press, 1967) pp. 67–8.
2. Distinguished anthropologist M. N. Srinivas used the term 'many-layered' society in connection with India so as to indicate her many layers of experience, including that of Westernisation. See his *Social Change in Modern India* (California University Press, 1966) p. 53.
3. I have used the term 'classical civilisation' to include both the Vedic period and the Sanskritic period, or what is often described as the classical period, in ancient Indian history.
4. M. Hiriyanna, *Outlines of Indian Philosophy* (London: George Allen & Unwin, 1932) p. 19.
5. Surendranath Dasgupta, *A History of Indian Philosophy*, vol. I (Cambridge University Press, 1957) *passim*, p. vii.
6. See in this connection 'Individuality and Equality in Hinduism' by A. H. Somjee in *Equality*, vol. IX, ed. J. R. Pennock and John Chapman (New York: Atherton Press, 1967).
7. S. Radhakrishnan, *Indian Philosophy* (London: George Allen & Unwin, 1927) p. 26.
8. U. N. Ghosal, *A History of Indian Political Ideas* (Oxford University Press, 1966) p. 5.
9. Ibid., p. 533.
10. One of the leading scholars of ancient Indian polity, Dr Altekar, wrote: 'Most of the dynasties in ancient India used to flourish for about two centuries. The village communities and councils were, on the other hand, of hoary antiquity and derived their powers from immemorial custom . . . ' Further, Sir Charles Metcalfe, the then Acting Governor General, wrote in 1830, 'The village communities are little republics, having nearly everything they can want within themselves, and almost independent of any foreign relations. They seem to last where nothing else lasts. Dynasty after dynasty tumbles down; revolution succeeds revolution; but the village community remains the same', quoted by Jayaprakash Narayan, *A Plea For Reconstruction of Indian Polity* (Rajghat, Kashi: Akhil Bharat Seva Sangh Prakasham) pp. 28 and 31, respectively.
11. P. T. Raju, *Idealist Thought in India* (Cambridge, Mass.: Harvard

University Press, 1953) pp. 378–9.
12. K. M. Panikkar, *The Foundation of New India* (London: George Allen & Unwin, 1963) p. 62.
13. See in this connection a fascinating work by K. M. Panikkar, *Asia and the Western Dominance* (New York: John Day, 1959) *passim*, pp. 18–19.
14. Louis Dumont, *Religion, Politics and History in India* (The Hague: Mouton, 1970) *passim*, pp. 55–8.
15. M. N. Srinivas, *Social Change in Modern India*, p. 54.
16. Milton Singer, *When A Great Tradition Modernizes* (New York: Praeger, 1972).
17. See in this connection Selig Harrison, *India: The Most Dangerous Decades* (Princeton University Press, 1960).
18. 'Caste and the Decline of Political Homogeneity' by A. H. Somjee, in *American Political Science Review* (September 1973).
19. 'Social Cohesion and Political Clientilism in the Kshatriyas of Gujarat' by A. H. Somjee in *Asian Survey* (September 1981).
20. See in this connection Myron Weiner, *The Politics of Scarcity: Public Pressure and Political Response in India* (University of Chicago Press, 1962); Lloyd I. Rudolph and Susanne Rudolph, *The Modernity of Tradition* (University of Chicago Press, 1967); and my critique of these works in 'Caste and Decline of Political Homogeneity' in *American Political Science Review* (September 1973).
21. For the details of this see A. H. Somjee, *Democracy and Political Change in Village India* (New Delhi: Orient Longman, 1971).
22. For an extended discussion on this subject see A. H. Somjee, *Political Capacity in Developing Societies* (London: Macmillan, 1982).
23. See for the complex process of attaining a normative–pragmatic balance A. H. Somjee, *Political Society in Developing Countries* (London: Macmillan, 1984), especially the chapter on 'Normative–Pragmatic Considerations in Political Involvement: The Case of India', pp. 78–124.
24. See for the details of this process, identified by means of a case study, 'Party Linkages and Strife Accommodation in Democratic India' by A. H. Somjee in *Political Parties and Linkages*, ed. Kay Lawson (Yale University Press, 1980).
25. See for the details of mass movement–party–mass movement cycle A. H. Somjee, *Democratic Process in a Developing Society* (London: Macmillan, 1979) pp. 151–3. Also see in this connection 'An Examination of the Socialist Concerns, Critiques, Agitations, and Organizational Attempts within the Indian National

Movement' by Geeta Somjee (unpublished PhD dissertation, MS University of Baroda, 1976).

26. See for Marx's unfinished attempt to develop the concept of class his *Capital: A Critique of Political Economy*, vol. III (Moscow: Foreign Languages Publishing House, 1959) p. 863.

27. Prominent among these are the writings of Max Weber, Ralf Dahrendorf, Bendix and Lipset, Tom Bottomore, etc.

28. Ralf Dahrendorf, *Class and Class Conflict in Industrial Society* (London: Routledge & Kegan Paul, 1958) p. 9.

29. *Karl Marx – On Colonialism and Modernization*, ed. Shlomo Avineri, p. 10.

30. The bulk of studies on Chinese politics are cast in highly generalised terms and, in recent years, they have resorted to denouncing each other's 'paradigms'. Chalmers Johnson expresses this as follows: 'the majority of researchers on PRC politics have been working within the wrong paradigms of analysis and even when they have adopted an appropriate paradigm they have restricted themselves to its mythical rather than operational dimensions', *Asian Survey*, XXII, 10 (October 1982) 919. As opposed to that there is now a growing body of literature brought out by expatriate Chinese scholars which brings to bear the depth of their understanding of the cultural and historical influences on Chinese politics. The bulk of these expatriate scholars cautiously avoid high-powered but misleading conceptual vocabulary.

31. Benjamin Schwartz expressed his views on this as follows: 'Both the cultural and what might be called "objective" heritage of the past may in the long run have more to do with the shape of China's future than Marxist–Leninist Communism as we have known it. If the Chinese state continues in some sense to be a communist state this communism may, in the long run, be "Chinese" in many significant ways.' *Communism and China* (Cambridge, Mass.: Harvard University Press, 1968) p. 11.

32. John K. Fairbank, Edwin O'Reishauer and Albert M. Craig, *East Asia: Tradition and Transformation* (Boston: Houghton Mifflin, 1973) *passim*, pp. 40–3. The '*li*' has been variously translated. While its literal translation is considered to be 'ritual', in the context of 'Confucian *li*', it can also mean 'reason, principle; the fitness of things' (Mathew's *Chinese–English Dictionary* (Cambridge, Mass.: Harvard University Press, 1966) p. 564).

33. 'Silent Aspect of China's Heritage' by Ping-ti Ho in *China's Heritage and Communist Political System*, ed. Ping-ti Ho and Tang Tsou

(Chicago University Press, 1968) pp. 7–11.

34. Ibid., p. 25.
35. 'Military Separatism and the Process of Reunification Under the Nationalist Regime, 1922–1937' by C. Martin Wilbur in *China's Heritage and Communist Political System*, p. 220.
36. Ibid., pp. 28–9.
37. 'Revolution, Reintegration, and Crisis in Communist China' by Tang Tsou in *China's Heritage and Communist Political System*, pp. 282–9.
38. Franz Schurmann made use of the conceptual difference between 'organisation' (goal-oriented and well disciplined) and 'institutions' (as integral parts of social relationships) as developed by Selznick. Such a distinction, nevertheless, did not effectively go to the heart of the matter. See for this distinction his paper on 'The Attack of Cultural Revolution on Ideology and Organisation' in *China's Heritage and Communist Political System*, p. 533. Also see his *Ideology and Organization in Communist China* (California University Press, 1968).
39. *Passim.*, pp. 537–41.
40. 'Chinese Kinship and Chinese Behavior' by Francis L. K. Hsü in *China's Heritage and Communist Political System*, pp. 581–2.
41. Ibid., pp. 594–600.
42. See in this connection John K. Fairbank, Edward O'Reischauer and Albert Craig, *East Asia: Tradition and Transformation*, p. 436.
43. Fei Hsiao Tung, *Towards A People's Anthropology* (Beijing, China: New World Press, 1981). In the words of the author: 'It is remarkable that, in spite of changes, there are still many nationalities in China today each having retained its own national characteristics', p. 27.
44. Byung-joon Ahn, *Chinese Politics and Cultural Revolution* (Seattle: University of Washington Press, 1976) p. 5.
45. James Chieh Hsiung, *Ideology and Practice: The Evolution of Chinese Communism* (New York: Praeger, 1970) p. 4.
46. Ibid., p. 5.
47. Ibid., p. 7.
48. Ibid., pp. 291–2.
49. A. Doak Barnett, *Uncertain Passage: China's Transition to A Post-Mao Era* (Washington, D.C.: The Brookings Institution, 1974).
50. One of the few scholars to get an opportunity in recent years to work on these lines was Steven W. Mosher, but unfortunately his approach and work became far too controversial. See, for

what it is worth, his *The Broken Earth: The Rural Chinese* (London: Collier-Macmillan, 1983).

51. See his 'The Attack of the Cultural Revolution on Ideology and Organization' in *China's Heritage and Communist Political System*, p. 533.

52. Thomas Smith quoted by Reinhard Bendix in 'Preconditions of Development: A Comparison of Japan and Germany' in *Social Change in Modern Japan*, ed. R. P. Dore (Princeton University Press, 1967) p. 33.

53. One of the major works on what could America borrow from Japan was Ezra Vogel's *Japan as Number One: Lessons for America* (Cambridge, Mass.: Harvard University Press, 1979).

54. Ibid., pp. 5–6.

55. R. P. Dore, *City Life in Japan: A Study of Tokyo Ward* (London: Routledge & Kegan Paul, 1958) p. 378.

56. Ruth Benedict's views quoted by R. P. Dore, ibid., p. 382.

57. Ibid., pp. 390–1.

58. See, for an interesting discussion of this problem, E. Wight Bakke, *Revolutionary Democracy: Challenge and Testing in Japan* (Hamdel, Conn.: Archon Books, 1968).

59. Ibid., p. 70. Also see in this connection 'Democratic Theories and Japanese Modernization' by F. Q. Quo in *Modern Asian Studies*, 6, 1 (1972).

60. In the field of political economy, there is a growing realisation on the part of some scholars that even in an era of post-industrial revolution, with the penetration of high technology in all segments of the economy, national decisions in Japan continue to be influenced by a number of historical and cultural conditions. In the words of Raymond Vernon 'The two countries [United States and Japan] could not have responded differently to similar problems. And in each case, with startling consistency, the responses seemed to stem from the distinctive aspects of each country's history and culture . . . ', *The Two Hungry Giants: The United States and Japan in the Quest for Oil and Ores* (Cambridge, Mass.: Harvard University Press, 1983) p. v.

61. E. Wight Bakke, *Revolutionary Democracy*, p. 14.

62. See in this connection Bradley M. Richardson, *Political Culture in Japan* (University of California Press, 1974) p. 8.

CHAPTER 4

1. *Politics and Change in Developing Countries: Studies in the Theory and Practice of Development*, ed. Colin Leys (Cambridge, Mass.: Harvard University Press, 1967) p. 7.
2. Gunnar Myrdal, *Asian Drama* (Harmondsworth: Penguin Books, 1967) vol. I, pp. 16–20.
3. Karl R. Popper, *The Logic of Scientific Discovery* (New York: Basic Books, 1961) pp. 40–3.
4. 'Relativism and Universalism' by Earnest Gellner in *Rationality and Relativism*, ed. Martin Hollis and Steven Lukes (Oxford: Basil Blackwell, 1982) p. 181.
5. 'Relativism, Rationalism and the Sociology of Knowledge' by Barry Barnes and David Bloor in *Rationality and Relativism*, ed. Martin Hollis and Steven Lukes, pp. 27–8.
6. Karl Mannheim, *Ideology and Utopia: An Introduction to Sociology of Knowledge* (London: Kegan Paul, Trench, Trubner, 1946) p. 2.
7. Quoted by Steven Lukes, *Essays in Sociological Theory* (London: Macmillan, 1977) p. 140.
8. Peter Winch, *The Idea of a Social Science* (London: Routledge & Kegan Paul, 1958) p. 100.
9. *Language, Thought and Reality: Selected Writings of Benjamin Lee Whorf*, ed. John B. Carroll (Cambridge, Mass.: MIT Press, 1966) p. 211.
10. Thomas S. Kuhn, *The Structure of Scientific Revolutions* (University of Chicago Press, Phoenix Book, 1965) p. 110.
11. Quoted by Steven Lukes, *Essays in Sociological Theory*, p. 142.
12. 'Relativism, Rationalism and the Sociology of Knowledge' by Barry Barnes and David Bloor in *Rationality and Relativism*, ed. Martin Hollis and Steven Lukes, p. 22.
13. Ibid., p. 27.
14. I am grateful to Henry Shue's work on *Basic Rights* (Princeton University Press, 1980) for the term 'moral minimum'. My own detailed treatment of the expanded term 'public minimum' is presented on pp. 123–6 of this chapter.
15. See in this connection 'The Limits of Development Research' by Paul Streeten in *World Development*, 2, 10–12 (Oct–Dec 1974) 14.
16. 'Social Determination of Truth' by Steven Lukes in *Modes of Thought: Essays on Thinking in Western and Non-Western Societies*, ed. Robin Horton and Ruth Finnegan (London: Faber & Faber, 1973) p. 230.

138   *Parallels and Actuals of Political Development*

17. Lucian W. Pye, *Aspects of Political Development* (Boston: Little, Brown, 1966) *passim*, pp. 33–7.
18. 'The Theory of Political Development' by Fred W. Riggs in *Contemporary Political Analysis*, ed. James C. Charlesworth (New York: Free Press, 1967).
19. 'The Development Syndrome: Differentiation–Equality–Capacity' by James Coleman in *Crises and Sequences in Political Development* by Leonard Binder, James Coleman *et al.* (Princeton University Press, 1971) *passim*, pp. 73–6.
20. Samuel P. Huntington and Joan Nelson, *No Easy Choice: Political Participation in Developing Countries* (Cambridge, Mass.: Harvard University Press, 1976).
21. See for the details of this process A. H. Somjee, *Political Capacity in Developing Societies* (London: Macmillan, 1982) pp. 2–4, 17–28.
22. See for the nature of impediments to the growth of political capacity in India, Japan, Mexico, Nigeria and Yugoslavia, A. H. Somjee, ibid., pp. 29–59, 60–90.
23. Henry Shue, *Basic Rights*.
24. See in this connection 'The Theory and Practice of Political Resistance' in A. H. Somjee, *Political Society in Developing Countries*, pp. 110–124.

Index

140   *Index*

Gellner, Earnest, 105, 113
Gujarat, 23

Hancock, Marlene, 131n
Harris, Marvin, 129n
Harrison, Selig, 133n
Hartz, Louis, 130n
Hermassi, Elbaki, 127n, 128n
Hiriyanna, M., 132n
Hollis, Martin, 137n
Horton, Robin, 30, 129n
Hsü, Francis L.K., 135n
Hume, David, 29
Huntington, Samuel, 119, 138n

Iberic-Latin, 56, 59
India: classical civilisation and
  political norms, 63–5;
  democratic process, 72–9;
  panchayats, 65; plurality,
  contradictions, coexistence in
  philosophical thought, 70–2;
  social and religious reform
  movements, 68–71;
  syncretic capacity, 70
Inkeles, Alex, 8–9, 34, 128n, 130n
Islam: state and religion, 53–4;
  Wahhabistic Islam, 53–4

Janata movement, 82
Japan, viii; group-fused individuals,
  97–8; group cohesion, 95–8;
  imposed democratic institutions,
  98–101
Jinnah, 43
Johnson, Chalmers, 134n

Kant, Immanuel, 71, 110
Kenya, 50–1
koketai, 100
Kuhn, Thomas, 114–15, 137n
Latin American scholars, 55–8
Lawson, Kay, 133n
'leader society' and 'follower society',
  1
Leiden, Carl, 131n
Lerner, Daniel, 6, 127n, 128n
Levine, Robert A., 128n
Levy, 34, 98

Lévy-Bruhl, 26, 29
Leys, Colin, 137n
Liaquatali Khan, 43
Lipset, S.M., 134n
Lukes, Steven, 137n

Maine, 33
Malinowski, B., 28, 129n
Malloy, James M., 131n
Mannheim, Karl, 113–14, 137n
Marx, Karl, 3–4, 26, 35, 71, 82,
  133n, 134n
Mehsana, 22
Mennell, Stephen, 130n
modernity 7–9; block borrowing, 35;
  borrowing and grafting, 37
Montesquieu, 27
Moore Jr, Barrington, 6, 127n
Morgan, 28
Morris-Jones, 62
Mosher, Steven W., 134–5n
Mujib, 45
multilayered political societies, viii;
  India, China, Japan, 60–1;
  conceptual inadequacy in studying
  their peculiarities, 79–85, 93–5,
  97–8, 99–101
Myrdal, Gunnar, 105, 137n

Narayan, Jayaprakash, 65, 84, 125,
  132n
Nelson, Joan, 119, 138n
nemesis of hypermodelling, ix
Nigeria, 51
Nisbet, Robert, vii, 36–7, 130n;
  Weber's fallacy of emanationism,
  37

O'Reishauer, Edwin, 134n, 135n
Organski, 6, 127n

Paine, Margaret, x
Pakistan, 43–5; search for a *rechstaat*,
  43; state and religion, 43–4
Panikkar, K.M., 107, 133
parallels, vi, 111–12
Pareto, 11
Parsons, Talcott, 6, 14, 127n;
  'pattern variables', 11–12

Ping-ti Ho, 134n
Popper, Karl, 105, 129n, 137n
postulates, 109–11
Powell, Bingam, 19, 129n
'public minimum', ix, 123–5
Pye, Lucian, 12, 21–5, 118, 119, 129n, 138n

Quo, F.Q., 136n

Radcliffe-Brown, 11, 28–9
Raju, P.T., 132n
relativism and universalism in political development, 102–4, 117–26
Richardson, Bradley M., 136n
Riggs, F.W., 118, 130n, 138n
Rosenburg, Bernard, 130n
Rostow, W.W., 6, 127n
Rudolph, Lloyd and Susanne, 133n

samurais, 95, 100
satyagrahic, 84
Saudi Arabia, 53–4
Schumpeter, 37; unassimilable borrowing, 41, 95
Schurmann, Franz, 135n
Schwartz, Benjamin, 134n
Schweinitz, Karl de, 79
Shils, Edward, 19, 128n
Shue, Henry, 137n, 138n
Singer, Milton, 70
Smith, David, 8–9, 128n, 130n
Socrates, 110
Somjee, A.H., 131n, 132n, 133n, 138n
Somjee, Geeta, 134n
Spencer, 34, 35
Sri Lanka, 46–8; Tamils, 46–7
Stone, John, 130n
Streeten, Paul, 127n, 137n

Sumner, 9

Tang Tsou, 134n, 135n
Tawney, R.H., 130n
Textor, 6
Tocqueville, Alexis de, 16, 37, 41, 130n; revolutions and different degrees of social change, 38
Toennis, 34
Tung, Fei Hsiao, 135n
Turkey, 53–5

universalistic assumptions, 1, 2, 5
unrefined theory, 104–6
universalistic and relativistic position, vii-ix

Veblen, T., 37, 95; borrowing from other societies, 40–1
Veliz, Claudio, 131n
Verba, Sidney, 16–18, 128n
Vernon, Ray, 136n
Vogel, Ezra, 128n, 136n

Weber, Max, vii–viii, 12, 16, 34, 41, 59, 79, 130n, 134n; differences between societies, 38–40; fallacy of emanationism, vii
Weiner, Myron, 133n
Western, vi
Western bias, vii
Western Europe, viii
Western state system, 1
Whorf, 114
Wiarda, Howard, 127n, 131n
Wilbur, C. Martin, 135n
Winch, P., 114, 137n
Wittgenstein, 110